# The Silence of Divine Love

# The Silence of Divine Love

BRENDAN SMITH

Foreword by
Cardinal Basil Hume

Una palabra habló el Padre, que fué su Hijo, y esta habla siempre en eterno silencio, y en silencio ha de ser oida del alma.

St John of the Cross: *Maxims on Love 21*

*(The Father spoke one word, which was his Son, and this [word] he always speaks in eternal silence, and in silence it must be heard by the soul.)*

Would he have the strength to endure the sufferings now in store for him? . . . A terrible anguish rose up in his heart . . . 'Lord why are you silent? Why are you always silent?'

Fr Rodrigues in *Silence* by Shusaku Endo

DARTON · LONGMAN + TODD

First published in 1998 by
Darton, Longman and Todd Ltd
1 Spencer Court
140–142 Wandsworth High Street
London SW18 4JJ



ISBN 0–232–52245–6

A catalogue record for this book is available from the British Library.



Thanks are due to the following for permission to quote copyright material: A.P. Watt Ltd on behalf of Michael Yeats for 'The Tower', 'Sailing to Byzantium' and 'A Prayer for Old Age' taken from *The Collected Poems of W.B. Yeats*; Faber and Faber Ltd for 'Anthem for St Cecilia's Day' by W.H. Auden taken from *Collected Poems* and 'Little Gidding' and 'East Coker' by T.S. Eliot taken from *Collected Poems 1909–1962*; Penguin Books for '7 Lachrimae amantis' taken from 'LACHRIMAE, or Seven tears figured in seven passionate Pavans' first published in *Tenebrae* in *Geoffrey Hill: Collected Poems* (copyright Geoffrey Hill, 1978, 1985); Macmillan General Books for 'Amen', 'Via Negativa', 'The New Mariner', 'The Absence', 'The Kingdom' by R.S. Thomas taken from *Later Poems: A Selection 1972–1982.*

Designed by Sandie Boccacci
Phototypeset in 10.75/14 pt Adobe Caslon Regular by Intype London Ltd
Printed and bound in Great Britain by
Redwood Books, Trowbridge, Wiltshire

With love and gratitude
to Jen and to the Ampleforth Community

# Contents

# Acknowledgements

I wish to express my special thanks to Abbot Luke Rigby for his encouragement to seek publication, to Judith Lang for her constant interest and helpful suggestions, and, above all, to my wife Jen for her limitless patience and care in typing all the text.

# Foreword

BRENDAN SMITH HAS been a life-long friend. For that reason alone I would wish to commend this book. There is, of course, a much more important reason. *The Silence of Divine Love* is a significant contribution to that search for God which we should all undertake. But can we find God or can we not?

If we can, then what is the mode of our searching? Brendan Smith uses his knowledge of the poets, particularly Dante, to help him find concepts and words to try to express the inexpressible. His background as a mathematician provides him with another instrument for his task, as does, of course, his own life experience.

The heart of the argument, as I understand it, is that we encounter hints of the numinous in different situations. We do so in the writings of the poets, but especially in silence, in a world where words have no place. Silence, however, can sometimes seem oppressive. In prayer it can make us feel empty and alone. We may be tempted to give up altogether. But there is a deep paradox here. The author writes:

'Without God we are nothing. But paradoxically the emptiness which we experience in prayer is also the beginning of the fullness of being for which we are destined in the final union with our creator.'

It is only by entering into the void that we begin to find God. And is it not true that it is God who searches for us and in our poverty and frailty discovers us?

For my part, the experience of emptiness and darkness is a

precious, yet painful, moment in the search for God. It is, though, greatly consoling to know that we can meet him who is 'the way, the truth and the life' and whom to see is to have known the Father. I think Brendan would agree.

His book is a deep and serious one. It explores the mysteries of our human existence in a perceptive way, and I commend it to all those who seek after the truth.

Basil Hume

# Introduction

Je ne puis approuver que ceux qui cherchent en gémissant.
*(I can approve only of those who seek with groans.)*

Pascal

MUCH OF THIS BOOK is concerned with paradoxes of reality: the transience of earthly human existence and its eternal value; the empty void which can also be fullness of life; human suffering and God's love; the diminishments of age which may yet be the completion of growth; and – at the centre of it all – the mystery of the dereliction of the cross.

Some apparent paradoxes arise because we are looking at one part of reality from two different points of view. But this is not always the case; and we may wonder whether there are not true paradoxes *within* reality. Do they appear to us only because we have an incomplete picture, or is there paradox at the very heart of existence? Most of those in the West, whose thought-patterns depend so much on the Greek tradition since Plato, would say that it must be the former, since for them it is inconceivable that a statement and its negation could both be true at the same time. But this conviction is not as universal as it may seem to us. We have only to consider some Presocratic philosophers or Eastern religious traditions.

I am no longer sure that logical consistency is a universal law. I have a deepening conviction that there is, in some sense, irreducible paradox within reality. There are many other paradoxes besides those I have already mentioned; for instance, the transcendence and immanence of God; that it is by losing our life that we find it; love which is indistinguishably both giving and taking; the consciousness of free will and genetic or environmental conditioning; the paradoxes arising from quantum mechanics. It is interesting that in recent years a number of attempts have been made to build up systems of formal logic in which the principle of non-contradiction is discarded in one way or another without, it is claimed, causing logical chaos or collapse. Some logicians say that such an attempt is doomed to failure; but I am intrigued that reputable logicians have claimed to produce such systems, because this would accord well with the way I feel about the nature of reality. In the mathematical theory of functions there can occur what are called 'singularities', isolated points at which a function is not 'well behaved'. Physicists, too, speak of singularities in space-time, such as black holes. Is it possible that something similar occurs in the logic of reality: 'singularities' where the usual law of non-contradiction does not hold? After all, within standard logic itself there are similar isolated 'points', namely the logical paradoxes. There is, for example, the case of the village barber who claimed that he shaved all the men in the village who did not shave themselves and no others. What of the barber? If he shaved himself, then he did not shave himself; but if he did not shave himself, he did shave himself. It is true that logical rules have been constructed to 'by-pass' specific types of paradox, but others always seem to arise. If such linguistic paradoxes occur, perhaps there are also ontological paradoxes in existent reality.

In this book there is much quotation from the poets. It is strange that often the most effective way of trying to describe reality is through symbol and metaphor: we try to light up one aspect of reality by making connections with other aspects. For physical science this is generally through the 'metaphors' of mathematical models. As the physicist, Robert Shaw, has put it: 'You don't see something until you have the right metaphor to let you perceive it.' For the world of human experience poetry uses symbol and metaphor in their more usual sense. 'Figurative discourse is dense but opaque; conceptual discourse is clear but shallow' (Paul Ricoeur, at the World Congress of Philosophy, Brighton 1988). Since what the poet has to say can only be fully appreciated in his or her words, verse is presented here in its original language, with literal prose translations appended.

I readily admit to self-indulgence in introducing at various points miscellaneous details which interest me: I hope that they may be of interest to others also. Sir Thomas Browne similarly excuses himself for digressions in his letter to the dedicatee of *The Garden of Cyrus* (1658): 'Such discourses allow excursions, and venially admit of collateral truths, though at some distance from their principals. Wherein, if we sometimes take wide liberty, we are not single, but err by great example.' And he adds a side-note to 'great example': 'Hippocrates *On Superfetation* and *On Dentition* digresses on sexual intercourse and tonsillitis.'

Most of us who call ourselves Christians are only partially christianized. I am thinking not only of the will which sometimes makes unchristian choices, nor even of conscious attitudes and outlook. Although we have been fully redeemed by Christ, there are some dark places where his light does not seem to shine, with the result that in our deepest experience there is polarity, a polarity which will be a main theme of the pages that follow. These are intended as a starting-point for the reader's own reflections. In the end, all words are inadequate, even the poet's. We come nearest to understanding when we allow them to resonate into silence.

# 1

## The Rays of the Sun

Ognuno sta solo sul cuor della terra
trafitto da un raggio di sole;
ed è subito sera.

*(Everyone stands alone on the heart of the earth/ pierced by a ray of the sun;/ and all at once it is evening.)*

And we are put on earth a little space
That we may learn to bear the beams of love.

HERE ARE TWO SHORT texts that invite comparison. The first is an early poem by Salvatore Quasimodo (1901–68). He was a Sicilian, one of the so-called 'hermetic' Italian poets who wrote between the wars. There is, however, nothing obscure in this little poem. It expresses what we all surely feel at times: the essential solitariness of the individual, the piercing beauty of this world we live in, the tragic brevity of life, and – by implication – its ultimate meaninglessness.

For each of us life is but an instant in the inexorable passage of time; each of us just a speck of dust lit up for a moment in a sunbeam. In the context of the immensity of the physical universe and of the unimaginable aeons of time, the life of the individual seems trivial and pointless. Every human being stands alone in this vast, cold universe. On the other hand, there is also the experience of the great things of life: the beauty of nature and of art, the warmth of love and of friendship, the stimulus of challenge, the fulfilment of potential. There is so much that can fill us with joy. Sunlight through beech leaves, a Beethoven slow movement, certain lines of poetry: these are things that almost make one cry out with pain at their beauty; and, greater than these, there is the deep happiness that can come to us through human relationships. And so, in the Quasimodo poem, each human being is bathed in the warm sunlight of the joys and beauties of life. There is a brief splendour – and then, in no time, it is evening. Darkness falls. There is the tragic transience of beauty and of the individual human life. In the end it is all meaningless. Such thoughts lie behind the sadness which pervades Mahler's *Song of the Earth*, reaching its climax in the final song 'The Farewell'. After more than forty years, I can still hear Kathleen Ferrier's voice fading away on the repeated *ewig . . . ewig*, accompanied by the cold tinkle of the celesta: 'Everywhere the lovely earth blossoms into spring and grows green again. Everywhere and for ever the distant spaces shine blue . . . for ever . . . for ever.'

'The eternal silence of these infinite spaces frightens me.' Already in the seventeenth century Pascal was expressing what so many feel today. Living at a time when telescope and microscope had recently been invented, Pascal saw the human race 'caught between two infinities', the infinitely large and the infinitely small. He saw that the vastness of space was far beyond the range of our imaginations; and he also had a mathematician's intuition of 'the procession to the infinitesimally small', which was to lead in the next generation to Newton's and Leibnitz's invention of the calculus. In this day of radio telescopes, electron microscopes and subatomic physics, we too sometimes feel like Pascal's lonely individual, 'terrified at seeing himself between the two abysses of the infinite and nothingness . . . equally incapable of seeing the nothingness from which he comes and the infinite in which he is engulfed' (*Pensées* 72 edited by Brunschvicg).

As has often been remarked, Pascal can seem extraordinarily 'contemporary'. In the *Pensées* he makes his searcher after the meaning of life say:

> 'When I consider the brief span of my life, absorbed in the eternity that precedes and follows it, the little span that I occupy . . . plunged in the immensity of the spaces which I do not know and which do not know me, I am terrified and astonished to find myself here rather than there; for there is no reason why I should be here rather than there, why now rather than then. Who put me here? By whose order and plan were this place and time destined for me?' (*Pensées* B205)

This is the burden of Sartre's novel *La Nausée*, written in 1938. For Roquentin, the narrator, life had no meaning. He was tormented by the very *fact* of existence, especially of his own existence. Then one evening, sitting on a bench in a public park, he had an 'illumination'. Gazing at the exposed root of a chestnut tree, he suddenly experienced directly what existence was. Back in his room and reflecting on this experience, the word 'absurdity' came into his mind. What he had experienced in the park was that all things around him and he himself were simply a collection of existing things which had no reason for their existence. Now he understood the key to existence: absolute absurdity. 'I had experienced the absolute: the absolute or the absurd.' Existence was absurd because there was no reason why anything should be or should not be. Things were 'just there', totally contingent, totally dependent – but dependent on nothing.

Before making any comment on Roquentin's conclusion that all existence is absurd, I want to return to the other two lines of verse which I quoted at the very beginning. They come from William Blake's 'The Little Black Boy'. As he and his mother look at the rising sun, she explains to him that God gives his light and warmth to all living things. The body, black or white, is 'but a cloud' which shades the soul until it has learned 'the heat to bear'. Then

> The cloud will vanish we shall hear his voice,
> Saying: come out from the grove my love and care,
> And round my golden tent like lambs rejoice.

Not only does God love the black boy as much as the white; but, precisely because of the colour of his skin, the black boy will learn sooner 'to bear the beams of love'; and so, in the last stanza, he says of the white boy:

> I'll shade him from the heat till he can bear,
> To lean in joy upon our Father's knee.

In the two poems that I have considered the human situation is evoked in strikingly similar imagery. Every human being is destined for a brief stay on earth, picked out in the rays of the sun. But how different is the effect. Probably the first thing that strikes us in Blake's words is the use of 'bear' in connection with 'the beams of love'. We have to learn to bear the heat of God's love. This idea is even more explicit in the lines of the devotional hymn writer, Isaac Watts, which Blake must have had in mind:

> Nor is my soul refin'd enough
> To bear the Beaming of his Love,
>     And feel his warmer Smiles.
> When shall I rest this drooping Head?
> I love, I love the Sun, and yet I want the Shade.
>
> (*Horae Lyricae*, 1764; 'Grace Shining' iv)

Before we shall be capable of experiencing God's love directly in the next life, we have to learn to experience it indirectly in this life. Glossing the poet's lines, we can say that we have to learn to accept that we are accepted by God. Herein lies the mystery of God's love: he loves me *as I am*, not as I ought to be. The gratuitousness of God's love is a major theme in St Paul and in the first letter of St John. One would think that this should be a cause for great joy and gratitude on the part of human beings, and indeed it is; and yet it is not easy to learn to accept that divine acceptance. I must be aware of my dark side and glad that God sees it; and I have to have the courage to accept that, seeing it, he nevertheless loves me, even to Calvary.

Bearing the beams of love can also be painful in human relationships. In unconditional human love there is the analogous happiness of being totally accepted without fear of rejection because of any fault or weakness, and of reciprocating such acceptance; but it can be very demanding, for it makes a person vulnerable, and there is no knowing what it may require of him or her in the vicissitudes of life. Similarly, our response to God's love for us may lead to burdens of responsibility. After St John in his first letter has spoken about God's gratuitous love for us, which he showed in the incarnation, he goes on, 'since God has loved us so much, we too should love *one another*' (1 John 4:11). Our response to God's love for us must be to love one another; and we do not know what that may involve. The responsibility of answering love with love can lead to suffering. Accepting God's love entails loving the world which he has created and loves. Love is a risk, and being open to love is to be open to change.

*

Quasimodo's poem expresses the utter loneliness of every individual, the transience of life on this beautiful earth, and its ultimate purposelessness. The other attitude is positive: life does have a purpose, though it is one whose end is not easily attained. It is to accept being loved, to reciprocate that love, and to have the courage to face whatever that may involve. There is also the implication that, if God loves us, then each of us has a quasi-infinite value. Indeed, the experience of human love itself persuades us of the immense value of the other person, and therefore of ourselves.

Which of the two outlooks corresponds to the reality of human existence? It might be expected that a Christian would answer: the second. But I maintain that *both* reflect profoundly true aspects of the human condition. In the history of this immense cold universe each of us *is* but a transitory speck, soon forgotten. There is no denying my littleness nor the extreme improbability of my existing at all. For one brief moment in time matter happens to have arranged itself so that I am here in existence. As Roquentin says in Sartre's novel, 'the essential is contingency . . . To exist is simply to be there, without any reason'. He goes on to say that some have tried to overcome the absurdity by inventing a necessary being, but no necessary being can explain existence: contingency is the absolute, perfect gratuitousness; there is no reason why anything exists or does not exist. Here, of course, Sartre, through his protagonist, is impugning one of the classical Thomist 'arguments from reason' for the existence of God. Whatever lack of cogency the alleged rational 'proofs' of God's existence may have, I cannot agree with Sartre, because it is precisely the *experience* of my contingency, of my essential dependence, that is a fundamental element in my belief in God. I shall be returning to this in later chapters.

I am, however, convinced that to feel what Quasimodo expressed in his short poem or what Sartre's Roquentin felt while sitting on the park bench is not, even for the Christian, a mere passing mood, but rather a profound human experience. It is a true part of being human to experience both the apparent meaninglessness of our brief contingent existence on this earth *and* the reality of eternal values. Some of those who have not felt profoundly one or the other can seem to lack a dimension. This is manifestly true of those who never reflect on the deeper things of life; but there are also some intelligent persons, sensitive to beauty and concerned about their fellows, who yet seem to lack a spiritual depth, perhaps because they have no sense of the transcendent. They are missing a faculty as others lack an aesthetic sense. On the other hand, we also meet sincere Christians who have never experienced the pain of the emptiness of insignificant human existence. It was sad to hear some years ago a priest-teacher say complacently after watching a performance of *End Game*: 'Well, I've got the measure of Beckett now', with the implication that Beckett expresses nothing but a superficial nihilism. A main theme of this book will be that the experience of what the Preacher of Ecclesiastes called the vanity (emptiness) of human existence is not just a passing mood of dejection but a deep reality of life. In fact, there is only one further depth: the happiness of knowing that we lie in the loving hands of God and that his love gives each of us eternal value. But this conviction does not necessarily remove the other, and I suggest that to be fully human is to experience both these things in tension.

Once again Pascal had the truth of the matter. In the *Pensées*, there is great emphasis on the wretchedness and the greatness of human beings, one of a whole set of Pascalian antitheses: the infinitely great and the infinitely small, the head and the heart, and so on. His primary point was the apparent contradiction between human wretchedness because of sin and human greatness as a creature loved by God and one with a sublime destiny. But, as Pascal saw it, human beings are also wretched because of their contingency, their unsatisfied desires, the void at the centre of their being which they try desperately to forget by constant activity and the seeking after pleasure. On the other hand, they have potential greatness through their possession of the power to know and to love, which gives them eternal worth and should bring them happiness and fulfilment. For Pascal these powers have been corrupted by original sin (which I shall consider in a later chapter); but God in his mercy has restored the human race through the death and resurrection of Jesus Christ. 'The greatness and the wretchedness of man are so evident that true religion must necessarily teach us both that there is a profound principle of greatness in man and that there is also a profound principle of wretchedness' (*Pensées* B430).

*

Of the two strands which I have picked out as implicit in Quasimodo's short poem, I suppose that sharp regret at the transience of beauty and of human life is more typical of nineteenth-century Romanticism, while anguish in the face of the meaninglessness of life reflects twentieth-century *Angst*. Much of the Sicilian poet's early verse is concerned with the loss of short-lived happiness and of beauty that can never be recovered. When he moved to Northern Italy and its winter mists, he thought of himself as exiled from the island which he wrote of as a lost garden of Eden and which, in its pervasive Greek inheritance, he saw as a symbol of eternal beauty. In this attitude there is still some degree of immaturity and self-indulgence; and Blake has the answer for those who cling to the inevitably transient:

> He who binds to himself a joy
> Does the winged life destroy
> But he who kisses the joy as it flies
> Lives in eternity's sun rise.

The death and destruction wrought by war brought Quasimodo to the realization that a yearning for ideal beauty was not sufficient. At first it seemed to him that song was no longer possible:

> . . . l'usignolo
> è caduto dall'antenna, alta sul convento
> dove cantava prima del tramonto.
> . . .
> la città è morta, è morta.

*( . . . the nightingale/ has fallen from the flag pole, high on the convent/ where he used to sing before sunset . . . the city is dead, is dead.)*

(I don't know whether the juxtaposition of the nightingale and the convent was a deliberate echo of 'Sweeney among the Nightingales'. Quasimodo published a number of translations from English, but none of Eliot's.) He was deeply anguished by the agony of witnessing the inhuman reprisals meted out to the Italian partisans by the Fascists and the occupying Germans after the Armistice in September 1943. He made use of Psalm 137 (136), the cry of the Jewish people in exile in Babylon, to express the sense of exile when one's own country is under foreign occupation.

> E come potevamo noi cantare
> con il piede straniero sopra il cuore,
> fra i morti abbandonati nelle piazze
> sull'erba dura di ghiaccio, al lamento
> d'agnello dei fanciulli, all'urlo nero
> della madre che andava incontro al figlio
> crocifisso sul palo del telegrafo?
> Alle fronde dei salici, per voto,
> anche le nostre cetre erano appese,
> oscillavano lievi al triste vento.

*(And how could we sing/ with the foreign foot on our heart,/*

*among the dead abandoned in the squares/ on the grass hard with ice/ to the lamb-bleat(s) of the children, to the black howl/ of the mother going towards her son/ crucified on a telegraph pole?/ On the willow-boughs, as an offering,/ our lyres too were hung/ (and) swayed lightly in the sad wind.)*

The horrors of war brought a new maturity to Quasimodo's poetry in the 1940s, no longer concerned with the self in its solitude but rather with compassion for the human family of which he was a member. Most critics, however, consider that later he lost a good deal of his poetic inspiration; and there was surprise in 1959 when the Nobel Prize for Literature was awarded to him, rather than to Ungaretti or Montale.

*

As for the other strand, anguish at the meaninglessness of existence, it has become widely accepted that many of contemporary Western neuroses stem from the inability to find any meaning in life. The psychotherapist Viktor Frankl, who had already before the war coined the word 'logotherapy' to describe his 'meaning-therapy', found his theories corroborated by his experience in a concentration camp. It became clear that, at the most fundamental level, survival was only possible for those who were aware of some meaning in life. As he says, even in this borderline situation, to remain a human being was open to decision, and there existed the possibility of holding oneself above the influence of one's environment. In less extreme circumstances, too, there is plenty of evidence for the psychological fragility of those who can find no meaning to existence. However, I am suggesting that this is not merely neurotic, but can also be a natural and valid part of human experience. Most of us live most of the time, not necessarily superficially, but taking our own system of values and our beliefs for granted, Christian or otherwise. Only occasionally do we descend, or are led, to our real depths; and my conviction is that there the two experiences of our insignificance and our eternal worth are very close.

This paradoxical duality of one's nothingness and one's value is sometimes experienced in a slightly different way. We can feel that our humdrum daily lives are really rather pointless. We are busy about many things, but our activities are of no more ultimate value than seem those of ants dashing around their ant hill. And when activity is much reduced, as for example it is for me now in retirement in the Welsh hills, it can sometimes seem that one just exists like a blade of grass bending in the breeze, and of no greater importance. From one perspective indeed a human life is not of much significance: birth, growth, death in the space of a few years. Yet that being is capable of loving and of being loved, and in consequence is of great value. If, then, just by existing I have such value, so too in its own way has the blade of grass. All creatures are of God's making, and we owe them all a great reverence. As I see it, we only have the right to use or destroy any of them according to a sort of 'law of sufficient reason'. The justifying reason may be fairly trivial in the case of something like a blade of grass, but it needs to become progressively more serious as we move up the scale of being. We, and all creation with us, have value simply because we exist:

> Die Ros' ist ohn' Warum, sie blühet, weil sie blühet,
> Sie acht 't nicht ihrer selbst, fragt nicht, ob man sie siehet.

*(The rose is without a 'why', it blooms because it blooms/ it pays no attention to itself, it doesn't ask whether it is seen.)*

So wrote the mystical seventeenth-century poet, Johannes Scheffler, known as Angelus Silesius. The gap between a blade of grass and myself is as nothing in comparison with that between my contingent being and the absolute being of God – and yet he has brought me into existence just in order to love me; indeed, it is his love that has made me.

*

Much of what I have been considering in this chapter is contained in Hopkins' great poem 'That Nature is a Heraclitean Fire and of the Comfort of the Resurrection':

Cloud-puffball, torn tufts, tossed pillows ¦ flaunt forth, then
  chevy on an air–
built thoroughfare: heaven-roysterers, in gay-gangs ¦ they
  throng; they glitter in marches.
Down roughcast, down dazzling whitewash, ¦ wherever an elm
  arches,
Shivelights and shadowtackle in long ¦ lashes lace, lance and
  pair.
Delightfully the bright wind boisterous ¦ ropes, wrestles, beats
  earth bare
Of yestertempest's creases; ¦ in pool and rutpeel parches
Squandering ooze to squeezed ¦ dough, crust, dust; stanches,
  starches
Squadroned masks and manmarks ¦ treadmire toil there
Footfretted in it. Million-fuelèd, ¦ nature's bonfire burns on.
But quench her bonniest, dearest ¦ to her, her clearest-selvèd
  spark
Man, how fast his firedint, ¦ his mark on mind, is gone!
Both are in an unfathomable, all is in an enormous dark
Drowned. O pity and indig¦nation! Manshape, that shone
Sheer off, disseveral, a star, ¦ death blots black out; nor mark
      Is any of him at all so stark
But vastness blurs and time ¦ beats level. Enough! the
  Resurrection,
A heart's-clarion! Away grief's gasping, ¦ joyless days, dejection.
      Across my foundering deck shone

A beacon, an eternal beam. ' Flesh fade, and mortal trash
Fall to the residuary worm; ' world's wildfire, leave but ash:
In a flash, at a trumpet crash,
I am all at once what Christ is, ' since he was what I am, and
This Jack, joke, poor potsherd, ' patch, matchwood, immortal diamond,
Is immortal diamond.

Hopkins wrote this difficult but magnificent poem, so full of explosive energy, in the summer of 1888, three years after the group of 'terrible' sonnets of desolation and some months before the final period of spiritual and emotional aridity and his death in 1889. He uses Heraclitus' belief that all nature is eternally in flux, together with the traditional four elements (earth, water, air and fire) of other presocratic philosophers. Air and water form the clouds, falling as rain to turn the earth into mud, which fire (the sun) and air (the wind) dry into dust; and then – it is implied – the moisture rises again to form new clouds. Thus continues the eternal cycle of nature, and in so doing produces all the wonderful beauty of the visible world, exemplified by white cumulus clouds racing across the sky, the lacy shadows of elm branches cast by strips of sunbeams on whitewashed walls, and the lovely effects of the wind, which, in drying the mud to dust, obliterates the footprints left by trudging men and women of toil.

In this ever renewed 'bonfire' of natural energy, each person's life is a mere spark, even though he or she is the most individuated of beings. Death blots each one out, and they are soon forgotten. In contrast to the eternally cyclic flux of nature, each individual ('disseveral') human being has only a linear descent into the darkness of dissolution. The thought of this tragic destiny fills us with horror and anger. But then the Christian remembers that this is not the end. Our fleshly lives in this beautiful world will soon fade away, leaving no trace behind;

but, petty beings as we seem to ourselves, we have a priceless and eternal worth because of Christ's life, death and resurrection.

*

When I see the heavens, the work of your hands,
the moon and the stars which you arranged,
what is man that you should keep him in mind,
mortal man that you care for him?
Yet you have made him little less than a god,
with glory and honour you crowned him.

(Psalm 8:4–6)

# 2

# The Abyss I

Abyssus abyssum invocat . . .

Psalm 42:7 (41:7)

*(Deep calls to deep . . .)*

BAUDELAIRE AND ST JOHN of the Cross were two great poets who both died in their forties. It might seem that they had little else in common; but in their poetry they share, in very different ways, something fundamental, which I shall discuss in this and the next chapter.

Charles Baudelaire was born in Paris in 1821, the child of his widowed father's second marriage. At the time of Charles' birth, his father was sixty and his mother twenty-eight. His father died when Charles was six; and there followed a very happy period of a year or so when he was the sole object of his mother's love. But in 1828 his mother remarried; and this was to have a disastrous effect on Baudelaire. His stepfather was always out of sympathy with him, and treated him, even in adulthood, with a total lack of understanding. Moreover, Charles bitterly resented that he had come between himself and his mother.

After being expelled from college for 'indiscipline', Baudelaire entered literary circles in Paris. He was supposed to be studying law, but he was only interested in literature. His stepfather disapproved of his feckless way of life, and sent him, when he was twenty, on a sea journey to the Indies. He probably did not go further than Mauritius; but the voyage and the exotic sights were to have a considerable influence on his poetic imagery. In 1842 he was back in Paris and had taken the mulatto, Jeanne Duval, a small-part actress, as his mistress. This liaison was to span twenty years, apart from a break of three years between 1852 and 1855. Jeanne was uneducated and a self-seeker, who was able to give Baudelaire only sensual pleasure. He was devoted and generous in looking after her material needs in later years when she was ill, in spite of her lack of gratitude.

By 1844 Baudelaire was heavily in debt through his dissolute life of drug-taking and involvement with prostitutes. He had no regular job, although he had already written a number of the poems which were to appear in *Les Fleurs du Mal* in 1857. His stepfather and mother had his money put into a trust providing monthly payments, which however were insufficient for his way of life; and this humiliation contributed to the deterioration into bitterness of his relationship with his mother. After his stepfather's death in 1857, Baudelaire resumed contact with his mother, and towards the end of his life he began to address her again as *tu*, instead of using the deliberately less familiar *vous*.

Baudelaire's first published prose work was the *Salon of 1845*, which was the beginning of his work as an art critic. (He was among the first to recognize the worth of Delacroix, Daumier, Manet and other painters.) This was also the year when he first attempted suicide. In 1848, the year of revolutions, he went to the barricades; but this seems to have been motivated more by bohemianism than by political conviction, since he was never interested in politics, nor was he truly sympathetic to the so-called 'lower orders'. By 1850 he was also beginning to show the effects of the syphilis contracted in early manhood.

In 1852 Baudelaire separated from Jeanne Duval, and on 9 December he posted his first anonymous poem to Mme

Sabatier, a beautiful, intelligent woman, who kept a salon frequented by famous literary figures. He set her up as a feminine ideal, indeed as an idol, and continued to write anonymous poems to her until 1857; but when she discovered who the author was and offered herself to him, he was outraged and disgusted.

During the first half of the 1850s Baudelaire published translations of Edgar Allan Poe, art criticism and a number of poems in literary journals. In 1857 his stepfather died, and in June he published his poems under the title *Les Fleurs du Mal.* There was an outcry from the *bien pensants.* He was prosecuted and fined; and six of the poems were condemned for obscenity. Perhaps in order to enlist her help in his trial, he revealed himself to Mme Sabatier, with the consequences already mentioned. 'A few days ago you were a divinity; now a woman,' he wrote to her in a letter mixing *tu* with *vous.*

Although Baudelaire's health began to deteriorate in 1858, he wrote a number of his greatest poems in the following year. The second edition of *Les Fleurs du Mal* appeared in 1861 with thirty-five additional poems. By now Baudelaire, suffering from the renewed effects of syphilis, was depressed and was tempted to end his life. During the next two years he wrote a few more poems, but he was now in decline. He went to Belgium in 1864 in the hope of improving his financial position by a lecture tour on poetry, painting and drugs; but he hated that country. By 1866 he was paralyzed. He returned to his mother in Paris in July 1867 and died on 31 August.

*

Charles Baudelaire was a man without a centre. He did not have an integrated personality, but swung from one stance to another throughout his life. It is not surprising that critics have held a wide variety of views about Baudelaire's fundamental position, from that of a Satanism of deliberately cultivated evil to a profound Catholicism. It seems clear, at least, that neither of these extreme views is valid. In fact, it is not possible to find any consistently held position. For example, evil certainly had a fatal attraction for Baudelaire; but, in the few places where his alleged Satanism appears (for instance, in *Les Litanies de Satan*), it seems to stem from a sort of Swinburnian posturing. On the other hand, he did have a profound sense of evil; and having inherited a Catholic conscience but without faith, he was tortured by a sense of sin and consequent self-hatred.

His ambivalent attitude towards women, too, is revealed in his poetry. There are erotic poems celebrating the purely physical pleasure he obtained from his 'Black Venus', Jeanne Duval, and poems addressed to Mme Sabatier ('the White Venus'), in which she is placed on a pedestal of superhuman goodness and beauty. Here we may compare the early stanzas of two poems (though the first may in fact refer to another woman than Jeanne Duval):

*Les Bijoux*

La très chère était nue, et, connaissant mon coeur,
Elle n'avait gardé que ses bijoux sonores,
Dont le riche attirail lui donnait l'air vainqueur
Qu'ont dans leurs jours heureux les esclaves des Mores.

Quand il jette en dansant son bruit vif et moqueur,
Ce monde rayonnant de métal et de pierre
Me ravit en extase, et j'aime à la fureur
Les choses où le son se mêle à la lumière.

Elle était donc couchée et se laissait aimer,
Et du haut du divan elle souriait d'aise
A mon amour profond et doux comme la mer,
Qui vers elle montait comme vers sa falaise. . . .

*(My darling was naked, and knowing my heart, she had kept*

*on only her sonorous jewels, whose rich splendour gave her the victorious air that Moorish slaves have in their days of happiness.*

*When, as it dances, it throws out its lively, mocking sound, this glittering world of metal and stone ravishes me into ecstasy, and I love to distraction those things in which sound is mingled with light.*

*So she was lying down and allowing herself to be loved, and from the height of the divan she smiled with pleasure at my love, deep and smooth as the sea, which rose towards her as towards a cliff. . . .)*

*Réversibilité*

Ange plein de gaieté, connaissez-vous l'angoisse,
La honte, les remords, les sanglots, les ennuis,
Et les vagues terreurs de ces affreuses nuits
Qui compriment le coeur comme un papier qu'on froisse?
Ange plein de gaieté, connaissez-vous l'angoisse?

Ange plein de bonté, connaissez-vous la haine,
Les poings crispés dans l'ombre et les larmes de fiel,
Quand la Vengeance bat son infernal rappel,
Et de nos facultés se fait le capitaine?
Ange plein de bonté, connaissez-vous la haine?

Ange plein de santé, connaissez-vous les Fièvres,
Qui, le long des grands murs de l'hospice blafard,
Comme des exilés, s'en vont d'un pied traînard,
Cherchant le soleil rare et remuant les lèvres?
Ange plein de santé, connaissez-vous les Fièvres? . . .

*(Angel full of gaiety, do you know the anguish, the shame, the remorse, the sobs, the anxieties, and the looming terrors of those frightful nights which squeeze the heart like a piece of paper that is crumpled? Angel full of gaiety, do you know the anguish?*

*Angel full of goodness, do you know the hate, the fists clenched in the dark and the tears of gall, when Revenge drums its hellish tattoo, and takes command of our faculties? Angel full of goodness, do you know the hate?*

*Angel full of health, do you know the fevers which, along the high walls of the drab poor-house, like exiles drag their feet, looking for the rare sun and moving their lips? Angel full of health, do you know the fevers? . . .)*

(The title refers to the doctrine of the 'treasury of grace', by which the merits of the saints are available to sinners; so the gaiety, goodness, health of Mme Sabatier compensate for the poet's anguish, hate and fevers.)

I think these lines exemplify a key factor in Baudelaire's character: his inability to *relate* to other people in a really personal way. His poems concerned with women are not truly love poetry but erotic poetry in which there is no expression of a relationship with a person, only an obsession either with a sensual object or with an idol. This failure to relate comes out also in the section of *Les Fleurs du Mal* on Paris, the great city. Although he expresses some pity for the unfortunates and for the outcasts of society and a sense of fellowship with them, yet he also feels disgust or sometimes a sort of detached interest, and there is little sense of real community with other human beings. In fact, Baudelaire was unable to get outside himself: he saw the external world reflected in his own self.

Much of this must have been caused by the traumatic experience of his father's death when Baudelaire was six, and by the intrusion soon thereafter of an unsympathetic stepfather into his close relationship with his mother. This feeling of having been betrayed and abandoned by his mother certainly affected his attitude towards women, whom he saw as either whores or angels. Baudelaire felt rejected and deprived of love; and this pain was increased in early manhood by the humiliation of having his financial affairs taken out of his own hands. Sartre asserts that Baudelaire never grew up. Certainly, much points to a permanent immaturity: the failure to relate to others, the erotic fetishism, the self-hatred, the way he saw all exterior reality reflected through his own ego.

In many ways Baudelaire was a pathetic figure. He destroyed himself, but not without an agony of guilt and bitterness. By the time he wrote the sketch of a preface for a third edition of *Les Fleurs du Mal*, he was beyond any desire to continue the struggle: 'to know nothing, . . . to wish nothing, to feel nothing, to sleep and to go on sleeping, that is today my only wish. Ignoble and loathsome wish, but sincere.' What gave dignity to his life and work was his honesty of vision. He never hid anything from himself; and, as a poet, he always held to his principle that art must depict life in its totality. Although it is difficult to see how some critics can maintain that he was a believing Christian, he certainly inherited a Christian moral sensibility, which increased his sense of guilt.

If Baudelaire showed continuing personal immaturity, there was no corresponding sign of immaturity in his best poetry. Poems that he wrote at the age of twenty-one are those of a mature poet. In fact, there was curiously little development in his poetry. Many of the early poems are not significantly different in style from those of his later years. Only the dates of publication of most of his poems are known; and some critics will judge a poem to have been written, say, by 1843 (when the poet was twenty-two), while others attach it to the late 1850s.

As a poet, Baudelaire was classical in style, romantic in outlook. He often echoes the majestic language of Racine and writes in classical French verse forms. This can produce a striking contrast between the 'grand style' and the contents of his poems with their frequent sensuality, sordidness, bitterness and the exoticism of much of the imagery. He deliberately set out to produce a sense of shock in the reader, since he held that 'the beautiful is always strange'. Elsewhere he said that poetry consisted in drawing beauty from evil, a view reflected in the very title of his collection, *The Flowers of Evil*, though *mal* also retains its other meanings of pain and sickness.

One must, of course, beware of the fallacy of reading a poet's life into his poetry. One could hold that the *je* in a poem is no more the poet himself than the voice of the narrator in a novel is that of its author. But in the case of Baudelaire, it seems clear that a great deal of his direct experience is to be found in his poetry. In February 1866, just before he became paralyzed, he wrote, 'I have put into this terrible book [*ce livre atroce*] my whole heart, all my tenderness, all my religion (or parody of religion), all my hate'.

Throughout his life Baudelaire suffered much from what he himself described by the English word *spleen*. In English this now usually has a sense of ill-temper; but Baudelaire intended rather a lowness of spirit associated with a whole range of feelings from tedium to positive suffering and existential *Angst*. And here we are approaching what I am chiefly concerned with in this chapter. Baudelaire experienced acutely the emptiness at the centre of human existence. He tried to escape from it through sex, drugs and art; but all of these failed him. He sought in vain for an *évasion* from *le gouffre*, an escape from the abyss. As we shall see, this emptiness experienced in the depths of a human heart was not, for Baudelaire, just the emptiness of triviality, but the result of the inevitable frustration of humanity's infinite longings.

One sonnet actually has the title 'Le Gouffre':

Pascal avait son gouffre, avec lui se mouvant.
– Hélas! tout est abîme, – action, désir, rêve,
Parole! et sur mon poil qui tout droit se relève
Maintes fois de la Peur je sens passer le vent.

En haut, en bas, partout, la profondeur, la grève,
Le silence, l'espace affreux et captivant . . .
Sur le fond de mes nuits Dieu de son doigt savant
Dessine un cauchemar multiforme et sans trêve.

J'ai peur du sommeil comme on a peur d'un grand trou,
Tout plein de vague horreur, menant on ne sait où;
Je ne vois qu'infini par toutes les fenêtres,

Et mon esprit, toujours du vertige hanté,
Jalouse du néant l'insensibilité.
– Ah! ne jamais sortir des Nombres et des Êtres!

*(Pascal had his abyss, going with him everywhere. Alas, everything is a void – action, desire, dreams, words! And through my hair standing on end I often feel the wind of Fear.*

*High and low, everywhere the depth, the sandy shore, the silence, the terrible and bewitching emptiness. On the backcloth of my nights God with his skilful fingers draws a multiform and unrelenting nightmare.*

*I fear sleep as one fears a great hole, full of looming horror, leading one does not know where; I can see nothing but the infinite through every window,*

*And my mind, always obsessed with the fear of height, envies the insensibility of nothingness. Ah! never to escape from Numbers and Beings.)*

This is a marvellous evocation of the experience of feeling oneself poised above a great void, the abyss that is within, which reminds us of Hopkins:

O the mind, mind has mountains; cliffs of fall
Frightful, sheer, no-man-fathomed.
('No worst, there is none . . .')

There is a particularly striking and sinister image in the second quatrain, while the last line of the poem expresses a desire to escape from existence, 'Numbers' being the Pythagorean concept of the multiplicity of the created world.

One may distinguish two main aspects of this experience of the void. First, and obviously, there is the terrifying emptiness at the centre of human existence, which can lead a person to feel a vertiginous sense of falling into an infinitely deep pit, or of descending an endless threatening dark stairway, as in a Piranesi engraving. So, for example, in 'L'Irrémédiable':

Un damné descendant sans lampe,
Au bord d'un gouffre dont l'odeur
Trahit l'humide profondeur,
D'éternels escaliers sans rampe,

Où veillent des monstres visqueux
Dont les larges yeux de phosphore
Font une nuit plus noire encore
Et ne rendent visibles qu'eux:

*(A damned man going without a lamp down the edge of an abyss whose smell betrays its damp depth, down endless stairs without banisters,*

*Where slimy monsters wait, whose great phosphorescent eyes make the night darker still and leave nothing visible except themselves:)*

This experience of the horror of the emptiness of life and of the emptiness within the human heart brings a desire for the cessation of existence, as we have already seen at the end of 'Le Gouffre'. This longing to be obliterated is expressed again and again; one poem has the title 'Le Goût du néant', the desire for nothingness:

Et le Temps m'engloutit minute par minute,
Comme la neige immense un corp pris de roideur;
Je contemple d'en haut le globe en sa rondeur,
Et je n'y cherche plus l'abri d'une cahute.

Avalanche, veux-tu m'emporter dans ta chute?

*( . . . And Time is engulfing me, minute by minute, as the endless snow (engulfs) a stiffening body; I look down from on high on the globe in its roundness, and I seek no longer the shelter of a hut.*
*Avalanche, will you take me with you in your fall?)*

But this infinite emptiness has another side to it, a second aspect of the Baudelairean void. It is caused by humanity's infinite longings: for happiness, for fulfilment, for beauty. So it was not just for the negative reason of trying to chase away ennui that Baudelaire took to drugs, sex and art. There was the positive desire to satisfy the infinite longing of his human heart. As a young man he had tried hashish, but this did not fill the emptiness; and he later recognized in his book, *Les Paradis artificiels*, that drugs merely isolate the individual and 'instead of leading to angelic heights, only turn a man into a beast'. Throughout his life he searched for fulfilment in his relationships with a number of women, but neither the sheer sensuality of Jeanne Duval nor his idealizing of Mme Sabatier brought lasting satisfaction.

Baudelaire concluded that the infinite longings of the human heart were doomed to be for ever unsatisfied; this too was an experience of the void. So, in a rather different sense from Pascal, there are for Baudelaire two infinities: the bottomless pit into which the poet often feels himself to be falling, and the infinite desire for happiness and fulfilment. The inevitable frustration of the latter is the cause of the former; so they are two aspects of the same human experience, which is described by the title 'Spleen et Idéal' of the first and longest section of

*Les Fleurs du Mal*. For Baudelaire, as for earlier French Romantics, *spleen* stood for the feelings of dejection and tedium in the human spirit, and by *idéal* he meant human aspiration towards a 'beyond' impossible of attainment.

One of the four poems specifically entitled 'Spleen' expresses the mood powerfully:

> Quand le ciel bas et lourd pèse comme un couvercle
> Sur l'esprit gémissant en proie aux longs ennuis,
> Et que de l'horizon embrassant tout le cercle
> Il nous verse un jour noir plus triste que les nuits;
>
> Quand la terre est changée en un cachot humide,
> Où l'Espérance, comme une chauve-souris,
> S'en va battant les murs de son aile timide
> Et se cognant la tête à des plafonds pourris;
>
> Quand la pluie étalant ses immenses traînées
> D'une vaste prison imite les barreaux,
> Et qu'un peuple muet d'infâmes araignées
> Vient tendre ses filets au fond de nos cerveaux.
>
> Des cloches tout à coup sautent avec furie
> Et lancent vers le ciel un affreux hurlement,
> Ainsi que des esprits errants et sans patrie
> Qui se mettent à geindre opiniâtrement.
>
> – Et de longs corbillards, sans tambours ni musique,
> Défilent lentement dans mon âme; l'Espoir,
> Vaincu, pleure, et l'Angoisse atroce, despotique,
> Sur mon crâne incliné plante son drapeau noir.

*(When the low, heavy sky weighs like a lid on the groaning mind, prey to persistent ennuis, and, embracing the whole circle of the horizon, it pours on us a dark day sadder than any nights;*

*When the earth is changed into a damp dungeon, in which Hope, like a bat, goes beating the walls with its timid wing and knocking its head against the rotted ceilings;*

*When the rain, spreading out its long trails, imitates the bars of a vast prison, and a silent crowd of loathsome spiders come to weave their webs in the depths of our brains,*

*Suddenly, bells swing furiously and fling into the sky a horrible howl, like wandering, homeless spirits beginning their stubborn wailing.*

*And long hearses, without drums or music, move slowly in procession through my soul; and Hope, defeated, weeps, and cruel tyrannous Anguish plants his black flag on my bowed head.)*

The first three stanzas of subordinate temporal clauses develop the theme of the human race's fundamental situation: ennui without hope. At the beginning of the fourth stanza there is a sudden change of tempo to evoke the angry energy of the sounding bells, an image of listless ennui becoming positive anguish; and finally the wonderful imagery of the last stanza, introduced by the lugubrious lengthening of its first line.

The vain longing for a state of blessedness often leads the poet to dream of faraway places and exotic lands. A good example of this comes in a poem which also demonstrates how Baudelaire failed to make real contact with the other person in his dealings with women. 'La Chevelure' begins:

> Ô toison, montonnant jusque sur l'encolure!
> Ô boucles! Ô parfum chargé de nonchaloir!
> Extase! Pour peupler ce soir l'alcôve obscure
> Des souvenirs dormant dans cette chevelure,
> Je la veux agiter dans l'air comme un mouchoir!
>
> La langoureuse Asie e la brûlante Afrique,
> Tout un monde lointain, absent, presque défunt,

Vit dans tes profondeurs, forêt aromatique!
Comme d'autres esprits voguent sur la musique,
Le mien, Ô mon amour! nage sur ton parfum.

J'irai là-bas où l'arbre et l'homme, plein de sève,
Se pâment longuement sous l'ardeur des climats;
Fortes tresses, soyez la houle qui m'enlève!
Tu contiens, mer d'ébène, un éblouissant rêve
De voiles, de rameurs, de flammes et de mâts;

*(O fleece, curling down to the neck! O locks! O perfume laden with indifference! Ecstasy! To people the dark alcove this evening with the memories sleeping in this hair, I want to wave it in the air like a handkerchief!*

*Languorous Asia and burning Africa, a whole faraway world, absent, almost dead, lives in your depths, aromatic forest! As other spirits sail on music, mine, O my love, floats on your perfume.*

*I shall go there where trees and men, full of sap, swoon slowly beneath the heat of those climes; strong tresses, be the swell that carries me away! O ebony sea, you contain a dazzling dream of sails, of oarsmen, flames and masts;)*

Neither in these verses nor in the four that follow is the poet concerned with the person, only with the effect that her hair has on *him*, with the dreams of evasion that it evokes, of escape from harsh reality to distant exotic lands.

In his longest poem, 'Le Voyage', Baudelaire expands this theme of men and women's search to satisfy their desire for the infinite under the figure of a journey, with its inevitable disillusionment. This is summarized in the first two verses:

Pour l'enfant, amoureux de cartes et d'estampes,
L'univers est égal à son vaste appétit.
Ah! que le monde est grand à la clarté des lampes!
Aux yeux du souvenir que le monde est petit!

Un matin nous partons, le cerveau plein de flamme,
Le coeur gros de rancune et de désirs amers,
Et nous allons, suivant le rhythme de la lame,
Berçant notre infini sur le fini des mers.

*(For the child, fond of maps and prints, the universe matches his huge appetite. Ah! how large the world is by lamplight! How small the world to the eyes of memory!*

*One morning we set out, our minds aflame, our hearts full of resentment and bitter desires, and we go on, following the rhythm of the waves, rocking our infinity on the finite seas.)*

Every glimpse of the promised land turns out to be a mirage:

Chaque îlot signalé par l'homme de vigie
Est un Eldorado promis par le Destin;
L'Imagination qui dresse son orgie
Ne trouve qu'un récif aux clartés du matin.

*(Every island pointed out by the look-out is an Eldorado promised by Destiny; Imagination, preparing for an orgy, only finds a reef in the morning light.)*

All that the travellers learn from their journey is a bitter lesson:

Amer savoir, celui qu'on tire du voyage!
Le monde, monotone et petit, aujourd'hui,
Hier, demain, toujours, nous fait voir notre image:
Une oasis d'horreur dans un désert d'ennui.

*(Bitter is the knowledge which one gets from travelling! The small monotonous world, today, yesterday, tomorrow, always, shows us our own image: an oasis of horror in a desert of tedium.)*

Whether it is Keats' desire to fly away from 'the weariness, the fever and the fret', or Leopardi's conjuring up in his imagination of infinite space, a sea 'in which it is sweet to founder', the desire to escape from everyday life to a world of the imagination was a commonplace of Romantic poetry. (It is interesting, incidentally, that the Nightingale Ode and Leopardi's 'L'Infinito' were written in the same year 1819, when both poets were in their early twenties.) Moreover, as we have seen, Baudelaire remained in some ways personally immature. But these facts should not make us deny the validity of his experience of the void, both as emptiness and as desire. Great poet that he was, he was able to express in incomparable verse a profound aspect of the human condition. The negative experience that we have been considering in this chapter, together with the positive experience of unconditional love of another human being, are very nearly the deepest experiences that are open to the human person. But not quite.

# 3

# The Abyss II

Juan de Yepes was born not far from Avila in 1542. His father belonged to a wealthy family of silk merchants, but was cut off from them when he married a poor orphan girl, who was a weaver. He thus fell into poverty and had to learn to become a weaver himself. They had three sons, of whom John was the youngest, born only a few months before his father died. His mother moved to Medina del Campo where John received his elementary education, as well as working as an apprentice to local craftsmen. When he was seventeen, he began to work at the local plague hospital, whose superintendent offered to pay for his continued education at the Jesuit college in return for his work at the hospital. There he was given a thorough education in Spanish and classical languages and literature.

At the age of twenty John entered the Carmelite Order at Medina, taking the name of Juan de Santo Matía. After his novitiate and profession, he was sent to Salamanca for his philosophical and theological studies. He studied both at the Carmelite College and at Salamanca University, which at that time had a reputation to rival that of Paris or Oxford. John was ordained priest in 1567; and later that year he had his first meeting with St Teresa, who had come to Medina to arrange the foundation of her second convent of Carmelites of the Reform. She was fifty-two and John twenty-five. St Teresa at that time was thinking of extending the Reform to the Carmelite friars; and when John told her of his desire to become a

Carthusian for a life of solitude and contemplation, she persuaded him that he could find such a life in the Carmelite Order of the Reform.

St Teresa had been offered a small, derelict farmhouse in Duruelo as a first house for friars of the Reform; so John and one other went there in the autumn of 1568, to be joined soon after by three more. Thenceforward John was known as Juan de la Cruz. During the next few years the numbers of members and of houses of the reformed Carmelites increased rapidly. It was a return to the primitive rule; and as both nuns and friars of the Reform went barefoot, they were called Discalced. By 1575 the attitude of the Calced to the Discalced had begun to change, partly because of the tactlessness of Papal Visitors in favouring the Discalced over the heads of the Carmelite authorities. In due course the General Chapter of the Order resolved to suppress the houses of the Reform. In 1577 John of the Cross was arrested, taken to Toledo and told that, if he refused to renounce the Reform, he would be treated as a rebel. He did indeed refuse, and was imprisoned in a Calced monastery in a cell, ten feet long and six feet wide. It had no window, the only illumination being from a slit high up in the wall, so that John could only say his office by standing on a bench. It was freezing cold in winter and then suffocatingly hot during the Castilian summer. For nine months he was scourged three times a week and for the first six months he was allowed no change of clothing.

Throughout these terrible months St John of the Cross remained serene, even joyful, and wrote some of his greatest poetry. Eventually, taking advantage of a more lenient jailer, he became familiar with other parts of the monastery; and on 16 August 1578 he escaped by letting himself out of a window, using strips torn from a cloak. In October he was elected prior of the Discalced monastery of El Calvario in Andalusia. During the next few years, which were externally fairly calm, John held a number of administrative posts in the Order; but towards the end of his life, a new Vicar General of the Discalced turned against him. He was stripped of all offices and was sent to La Peñuela, a lonely priory in Andalusia, where he spent the last months of his life in almost continuous prayer, peaceful and happy despite great physical suffering from ulcers which spread over much of his body.

St John of the Cross was physically very small, only about five foot in height. When St Teresa was reporting the beginning of the Reform of the male Carmelites, she said she had 'a friar and a half' for the initial foundation. Kindred spirits though they were, Teresa and John had very different temperaments. It would be misleading to say that John was more austere, since they were equally austere in their way of life; but he was more naturally serious than Teresa and did not have her outstanding vivacity. This is not to say that he was in any way dour: the evidence of his brethren is that he was a lively member of any community.

The fact that John of the Cross was a mystic and a poet does not mean that he was impractical in daily affairs. For most of his religious life he held important positions of administration and responsibility for others. Nor do the austerities of his own life and his insistence in his teaching on the need for mortification imply any lack of appreciation of the goodness of God's creation. As we shall see in his poetry, he had an intense love of natural beauty, and he insisted that detachment from creatures simply bought a truer appreciation of them. When he was novice master or prior, he used to take his friars out into the country for relaxation; and he himself liked to go out into the solitude of nature to pray.

I am chiefly concerned with John of the Cross's poems and what they tell us about the theme of the abyss. Most Spanish critics are agreed that, by virtue of a handful of poems, he takes his place as one of the greatest poets in their language. A similar claim can hardly be made for his prose. The great bulk of his prose works are commentaries, written at a later date, on some of his poems. They form a classical exposition of Christian mystical theology; but there is little grace in their style. Clearly, St John of the Cross was not concerned to put any of the supreme artistry of his poems into his commentaries on them.

*

*Noche Oscura*

En una noche oscura, 1
con ansias en amores inflamada,
¡oh dichosa ventura!
salí sin ser notada,
estando ya mi casa sosegada.

A oscuras, y segura, 2
por la secreta escala disfrazada,
¡oh dichosa ventura!
a oscuras y en celada,
estando ya mi casa sosegada.

En la noche dichosa, 3
en secreto, que nadie me veía
ni yo miraba cosa,
sin otra luz y guía
sino la que en el corazón ardía.

Aquesta me guiaba 4
más cierto que la luz del mediodía,
adonde me esperaba
quien yo bien me sabía
en parte donde nadie parecía.

¡Oh noche, que guiaste, 5

oh noche amable más que el alborada:
oh noche, que juntaste
amado con amada,
amada en el Amado transformada!

En mi pecho florido, 6
que entero para él solo se guardaba,
allí quedó dormido
y yo le regalaba,
y el ventalle de cedros aire daba.

El aire de la almena, 7
cuando ya sus cabellos esparcía,
con su mano serena
en mi cuello hería,
y todos mis sentidos suspendía.

Quedéme y olvidéme, 8
el rostro recliné sobre el Amado;
cesó todo, y dejéme,
dejando mi cuidado
entre las azucenas olvidado.

*(1 On a dark night, fired with love's longings – oh happy chance – I went out unnoticed, my house now being stilled.*

*2 In darkness and secure, by the secret ladder [and] disguised – oh happy chance – in darkness and concealed, my house now being stilled.*

*3 On that happy night, in secret, for no one saw me nor did I look at anything, with no light or guide except the one that burned in my heart.*

*4 This guided me more surely than the light of noon to where one awaited me whom I knew well, in a place where no one was to be seen.*

*5 Oh night, you were the guide, oh night more lovely than the dawn, oh night that joined lover with beloved, the beloved transformed into the Lover.*

*6 Upon my flowering breast, kept wholly for him alone, there he remained asleep and I caressed him, and the fan of the cedars made a breeze.*

*7 When the breeze from the battlement parted his hair, with his serene hand he wounded my neck and suspended all my senses.*

*8 I stayed and forgot myself, I laid my face on my Beloved; all ceased, and I abandoned myself, leaving my cares forgotten among the lilies.)*

It is worth comparing this wonderful poem with Baudelaire's 'Les Bijoux' (p. 18). Both are written in the language of erotic imagery, of desire. In Baudelaire's poem the desire is simply for the pleasure, partly fetishistic, to be derived from the woman's body, without any question of a truly personal relationship; whereas John of the Cross is writing about the fulfilment of the desire to be totally united to the one who is loved. His poem has the descriptive subtitle: 'Songs of the soul that rejoices at having reached the height of perfection, which is union with God, by the path of spiritual negation'. It describes the journey of the soul to union with its God. The house of the senses has been stilled, and the soul goes forth with a joyful confidence which breaks into ecstasy in the fifth stanza with its almost obsessive repetition of the rich vowel sounds in the last two lines, followed by three stanzas describing the state of total union in love, using for the most part imagery of touch. It is possible that St John of the Cross wrote this poem during the terrible months in prison in Toledo. It was certainly already written only a short time afterwards.

What he undoubtedly *did* write in prison, as well as some minor poems, were the first thirty stanzas of 'The Spiritual Canticle', a poem chiefly inspired by the biblical Song of Songs. It takes the form of a dialogue between the Bride (the human soul) and the Bridegroom (God). At first the Bride is searching for her lover. She asks the woods and the meadows if he has passed their way, and receives the lovely answer:

Mil gracias derramando,
pasó por estos sotos con presura,
y yéndolos mirando,
con sola su figura
vestidos los dejó de hermosura.

*(Scattering a thousand graces, he passed through these groves in haste; and having gazed on them, with his image alone he left them clothed in beauty.)*

Then the Bridegroom appears, describing himself as a wounded stag, wounded with love:

Vuélvete, paloma,
que el ciervo vulnerado
por el otero asoma
al aire de tu vuelo, y fresco toma.

*(Return, dove; because the wounded stag appears on the hill, cooled by the wind and the freshness of your flight.)*

Now there is no more yearning, only the celebration of their union and the paradoxes of bliss:

La noche sosegada
en par de los levantes de la aurora
la música callada,
la soledad sonora,
la cena que recrea y enamora.

*(The tranquil night as it approaches the coming dawn, the silent music, the sounding solitude, the supper that refreshes and inspires love.)*

The spiritual marriage is now complete:

Entrádose ha la esposa
en el ameno huerto deseado,
y a su sabor reposa,
el cuello reclinado
sobre los dulces brazos del Amado.

*(The bride has entered the pleasant garden of her desire, and in delight she lies, her neck laid upon the gentle arms of her Beloved.)*

Now the Bridegroom bids all created things to cease distracting the soul.

It is truly astonishing that St John of the Cross could have composed this poem in the horrific conditions of his imprisonment. The first stanza perhaps reflects the appalling sense of abandonment by God as well as by men that he must sometimes have felt in his dark, narrow cell:

¿Adónde te escondiste,
Amado, y me dejaste con gemido?
Como el ciervo huiste,
habiéndome herido;
salí tras ti clamando, y eras ido.

*(Where have you hidden, Beloved, and left me moaning? You fled like the stag, having wounded me; I went out after you, calling; and you were gone.)*

The structure and much of the imagery of 'El cantico espiritual' is obviously modelled on the Song of Songs; but there are also traces of influence from Spanish secular poetry; and that John of the Cross was no naïve artist is clear, for example, from a stanza when the Bride, searching for her lover, bemoans his absence:

Y todos cuantos vagan,
de ti me van mil gracias refiriendo,
y todos más me llagan,
y déjame muriendo
un no sé qué que quedan balbuciendo.

*(And all those who rove about tell me a thousand graceful things about you, and all wound me more, and I-know-not-what which they stay and stammer leaves me dying.)*

In the last line he contrives to produce the effect of stammering with the triple *que* sounds.

At this point we may consider briefly the literary influences that lie behind John of the Cross's poetry, apart from the obvious one of the Bible. He uses the verse forms both of the popular songs of his time and of the cultured Italianate poetry introduced into Spanish a generation before by Garcilaso de la Vega. He uses the latter most notably in his three greatest poems: 'The Dark Night', 'The Spiritual Canticle' and 'The Living Flame of Love'. It is not certain how John came to be familiar with the poetry of Garcilaso and his friend, Boscán. Most seem to accept the hypothesis of the eminent critic, Dámaso Alonso, who suggests that John read these poets in his student days, and was later encouraged to model his own poetry on their techniques after he had read the religious versifier, Sebastián de Córdoba, who published a book of poems in 1575, in which he 'converts' the poetry of Garcilaso *a lo divino*; that is, he turns Garcilaso's secular love poetry into religious verse about the love between God and the human soul. John of the Cross used the same idea; but the great difference is that thereby he produced a group of masterpieces.

The great majority of St John of the Cross's extant prose works are commentaries on 'The Dark Night', 'The Spiritual Canticle', and 'The Living Flame of Love'. They have the same titles as the poems except for *The Ascent of Mount Carmel*, which is a treatise on the contemplative life (the ascent of Mount Carmel being taken as an image for the soul's ascent to contemplative union with God), arising from a commentary on stanza 2 of the poem, 'The Dark Night'. *The Ascent of Mount Carmel* and *The Dark Night* together cover nearly four hundred pages, although they only comment in detail on the first two stanzas of the poem; so clearly they are much more than commentaries. Although each was left unfinished, they form comprehensive treatises on Christian mystical theology. *The Spiritual Canticle* and *The Living Flame of Love* are on a less expansive scale and do form complete commentaries on their respective poems.

The reader who comes to these four prose works from the soaring ecstasy of the poems may at first be somewhat disconcerted. What was living image and symbol in a poem often seems to be given a laboured allegorical interpretation in the commentary. But further reading reveals a magisterial series of treatises on mystical theology.

The most fundamental image is that of the dark night. In chapter 2 of Book 1 of *The Ascent*, John explains that the journey to God can be called a dark night for three reasons. First, 'the individual must deprive himself of his appetite for worldly possessions. This denial and privation is like a night for his senses'. Secondly, the way itself, the road of faith, is like a dark night for the intellect. Finally, 'the point of arrival, God, is also a dark night to man in this life'. Later on (Book 2, ch. 5), he explains that the union with God which he is speaking about is not 'the substantial union' by which God is always present in creatures as their Creator keeping them in existence. It is rather what he calls 'the union of likeness', when the soul rids itself of all that is 'unconformed to the divine will and rests transformed in God through love'.

As already mentioned, the two commentaries on 'The Dark Night' cover only the first two stanzas of the poem, and are therefore chiefly concerned with the darkness of self-abnegation and of the way to God, rather than with the darkness of union with God in this life. The happiness of this union becomes the main theme of the commentaries on 'The Spiritual Canticle' and 'The Living Flame of Love'. In St John of the Cross's teaching, the way to God is certainly a way of negation; and his language can seem extreme and forbidding. But the motivation for undertaking this way is a positive burning love. The only purpose in the emptying of the self is to make space for God the Lover who is waiting to come. 'It should be known that if a person is seeking God, her Beloved is seeking her much more' (*Living Flame* 3,28). In his explanation of how the soul enters the dark night of sense (*Ascent* I 13), there are those 'instructions for climbing to the summit, the high state of union', some of which Eliot was to paraphrase in 'East Coker': 'To come to possess all, desire the possession of nothing. To arrive at being all, desire to be nothing. To come to the knowledge of all, desire the knowledge of nothing . . .'

Here we have the contrast which is so important to St John of the Cross: *nada/todo*, nothing/all. It is only by the way of nothingness that the finite human being can come to the infinite All of God. John sees the emptying of the intellect of all knowledge and the emptying of the will of all desire as prerequisites for attainment of union with God. 'A man makes room for God by wiping away all the smudges and smears of creatures, by uniting his will perfectly with God's; for to love is to labour to divest and deprive oneself for God of all that is not God. When this is done the soul will be illumined by and transformed in God' (*Ascent* II 5,7).

The only way of bridging the infinite gap between the soul and God, between Nothingness and the All, is by love. 'Love is the soul's inclination, strength and power in making its way to God, for love unites it to God' (*Living Flame* I 13). We should notice that this love, sublime as it is, has an erotic element in it. (It will be obvious that I am not using 'erotic' in its contemporary debased sense, but as meaning the love of desire, in contrast to agape, gift-love.) This element is evident in the poems; for instance in the second line of 'The Dark Night' ('fired with love's longings') or in the Bride's longing for the Bridegroom in 'The Spiritual Canticle'. John is even more explicit in his commentaries. Here are just three examples. 'This flame and enkindling increases to such an extent that the soul desires God with urgent longings of love' (*Dark Night* I, 11, 1). 'Any soul with authentic love cannot be satisfied until it really possesses God' (*Spiritual Canticle* 6, 4). 'The greater a person's love so much the more impatient is he for the possession of God, for whom he hopes at times with intense longing' (*Living Flame* 3, 22).

In order to have this desire for God one has to eliminate the desire for all that is not God. Hence the impression of forbidding austerity one may gain from reading John's mystical theology if one fails to understand the reason for his teaching on asceticism. Detachment from creatures is necessary for the freedom to be totally available to God. Once union with God has been attained, all else is found again in God. In the diagram he drew to illustrate the mystical ascent of Mount Carmel, John wrote, 'peace, joy, happiness: now that I no longer desire them, I have them all without desire'.

John's insistence on the need to rid oneself of all attachment to creatures is not a moral judgement but an existential principle that this is the only way to achieve union with God. In this he is completely in line with the non-Christian Neoplatonic tradition stemming from Plotinus in the third century. For Plotinus, too, the soul, purified by asceticism, ascends towards the One. 'All other loves than this he must despise, and disdain all that once seemed fair' (*Enneads* I 6, 7.). Even in his imagery, John follows the Neoplatonic tradition: the ascent to God by a ladder, the darkness, the polarity of Nothingness and All. John's mystical doctrine, however, is profoundly Christocentric. It is through a personal relationship with the historical Jesus that the soul can achieve transcendental union with God. John emphasizes throughout his writings that one makes spiritual progress only through the imitation of Christ and that everything is to be done for love of Christ. In his commentary on 'The Spiritual Canticle' he explicitly and repeatedly identifies the Bridegroom with Christ, the Word, the Son of God. Imitation does not mean following an external model, but implies a transformation into the likeness of Christ, as John makes clear in his amazing commentary on the line 'Let us see ourselves in your beauty' (*Canticle* 36):

> That I may be so transformed into your beauty that, being alike in beauty, we may see both of ourselves in your beauty, possessing now your beauty; in such a way that each looking at the other may see in the other his own beauty, since each are your beauty alone, I being absorbed into your beauty; and so I shall see you in your beauty, and you me in your beauty, and I shall see myself in you in your beauty, and you will see yourself in me in your beauty; and so I shall be you in your beauty, and you will be me in your beauty, . . . because your own beauty will be my beauty; and so we shall see each other in your beauty.

The mystic's loving union with God brings a knowledge which cannot be described. In the Prologue to the first redaction of his commentary on 'The Spiritual Canticle', John writes: 'Who can describe the understanding which he [God] gives to loving souls in whom he dwells?' He explains to Mother Ann of Jesus, for whom the commentary was written, that he cannot expound the stanzas adequately: 'For mystical wisdom, which comes through love and is the subject of these stanzas, need not be understood distinctly in order to cause love and affection in the soul'. This unitive love brings the dark knowledge of God about which John wrote in two poems, modified versions of the *villancico*, a type of popular verse. One (translated by Seamus Heaney in *Station Island*) is entitled 'Song of the soul that delights in knowing God through faith' and has the refrain *aunque es de noche* (although it is night) as the last line of every triplet, each of which also includes the word *sé* (I know). It begins:

> Que bien sé yo la fonte que mana y corre
> aunque es de noche.
>
> Aquella eterna fonte está escondida,
> que bien sé yo do tiene su manida,
> aunque es de noche.
>
> Su origen no lo sé, pues no le tiene,
> mas sé que todo origen de ella viene
> aunque es de noche.

*(For I know well the spring that gushes and flows, although it is night.*

*That eternal spring is hidden, for I know well where it has its abode, although it is night.*

*Its source I do not know, for it has none, but I know that all sources come from it, although it is night.)*

The other *villancico* ('verses written about an ecstasy of high contemplation') begins:

> Entréme donde no supe,
> y quedéme no sabiendo
> toda ciencia trascendiendo.

*(I entered where I did not know, and there remained unknowing, transcending all knowledge.)*

The last line, with its repetitive sounds, forms the refrain for the final lines of all eight subsequent seven-line stanzas.

These descriptions of an experience which is somehow beyond knowledge give us the impression that the mystical experience of union with God is so unrelated to any other that it cannot be adequately expressed in words, nor indeed even be 'known' in any ordinary sense. There seems to be here a discontinuity of experience. For most human beings perhaps the nearest analogy to such a discontinuity is in the climax of the act of love. It is not surprising that St John of the Cross should have used erotic imagery in his poetry. It provides the best approximation for describing the ineffable experience of mystical union with God.

I have spoken of the erotic element in the work of St John of the Cross because I have wanted to contrast his experience and his poetry with those of Baudelaire. Of course, the predominant element in Christians' love of God is agape, the loving offering back of their being to their Creator, an offering which is to be mirrored in their gift of themselves to others. It is this gift-love, which St Paul celebrates in 1 Corinthians 13: 'Love is patient and kind, love is not jealous . . . Love does not seek to have its own way'. Eros and agape are not two distinct types of love, but two elements in the one affective drive. By their very nature human beings seek happiness, desire fulfilment; but paradoxically they can only achieve that fulfilment by the gift of themselves. In particular, one of the wonders of human love is that the same act can be the expression both of desire and of gift.

The poem of John of the Cross which is entirely concerned with the bliss of mystical union is 'The Living Flame of Love':

*Llama de amor viva*

¡Oh llama de amor viva, 1
que tiernamente hieres

de mi alma en el más profundo centro!
Pues ya no eres esquiva,
acaba ya, si quieres;
rompe la tela deste dulce encuentro.

¡Oh cauterio suave! 2
¡Oh regalada llaga!
¡Oh mano blanda! ¡Oh toque delicado!
que a vida eterna sabe,
y toda deuda paga;
matando, muerte en vida la has trocado.

¡Oh lámparas de fuego, 3
en cuyos resplandores
las profundas cavernas del sentido,
que estaba oscuro y ciego,
con extraños primores
calor y luz dan junto a su querido!

¡Cuán manso y amoroso 4
recuerdas en mi seno
donde secretamente solo moras,
y en tu aspirar sabroso
de bien y gloria lleno
cuán delicadamente me enamoras!

*(1 O living flame of love, that tenderly wounds my soul in its deepest centre! Since now you are not aloof, finish now if you will; tear the veil of this sweet encounter.*

*2 O gentle cautery, O blissful wound, O soothing hand, O delicate touch that tastes of eternal life and pays every debt; by killing you have changed death into life.*

*3 O lamps of fire, in whose splendour the deep caverns of feeling, which were dark and blind, with rare beauty now give warmth and light together to their beloved.*

*4 How gently and lovingly you awaken in my breast where in secret you dwell alone; and by your sweet breathing, full of goodness and glory, how delicately you kindle me with love!)*

This union with God occurs at the deepest centre of the human creature's being. Indeed, in his commentary on the third line of the poem, John uses extremely emphatic language: 'The soul's centre *is God*. When it has reached God with all the capacity of its being and the strength of its operation and inclination, it will have attained its final and deepest centre in God; it will know, love and enjoy God with all its power' (*Living Flame* I, 12).

*

*Abyssus abyssum invocat*, 'deep calls to deep'. The early fourteenth-century German mystic, Meister Eckhart, uses the verse of the psalm which was quoted at the beginning of chapter 2 to illustrate the relationship between the empty abyss at the centre of our being and the depth of God's fullness. One can read 'deep calls to deep' in two ways: a human being's emptiness calling out to be filled by God, or God calling to his human creature, offering to fill that emptiness. The emptiness at the centre of his being that Baudelaire was always trying to flee (or to fill) was in fact the very *locus* in which the fullness of existence is to be found. Baudelaire tried to *escape* the horrors of this void through sex or drugs or the flight of the imagination to exotic lands; but these provided no answer to the ennui. St John of the Cross *sought* the void by the total emptying of all usual human desires, because that was the way to the fulfilment of the one supreme desire, union with his Creator at the centre of his being.

The Romantic poet tried in vain to transport himself in imagination beyond the reality of space and time; the Christian mystic was transported into a real relationship with the transcendent infinite. Baudelaire and John of the Cross descended to the ultimate depths of their respective abysses. Most of us are unlikely to follow them all the way; but unless we travel some way along *both* paths, we shall not have experienced fundamental aspects of being human. 'All creatures are balanced upon the creative word of God; above them is the abyss of the divine infinitude, below them that of their own nothingness' (Philaret of Moscow, nineteenth-century Orthodox theologian).

# 4

# The Mind in Love

La mente innamorata, che donnea
con la mia donna sempre, di ridure
ad essa li occhi più che mai ardea.

*Paradiso* xxvii 88–90

*(My mind in love, which is always in dalliance with my lady, burned more than ever to bring back my eyes to her.)*

As I shall be appealing to Dante quite frequently, it may be helpful to insert an introductory chapter about him. I have chosen the title and epigraph because the phrase 'the mind in love' is an apt description of the poet. Dante was a passionate man, passionate in his loves and in his hates, passionate also in his desire for knowledge and in the contemplation of truth. Dante Alighieri was born in Florence in 1265. The energy and genius of the Florentines, which produced such astonishing achievements in the arts, sciences and commerce over a period of more than three hundred years, led to very different results in internal political life during that same long period. Here there were constant divisions and struggles: struggles for power between leaders and between parties, and for the preservation of liberty by the populace. In the thirteenth century most of the city states of Northern Italy suffered from endless party strife between Guelfs and Ghibellines. These were nominally the opposing parties of Papacy and Empire, but in reality their adherents were often pursuing personal power or family vendettas. From the beginning of the century these party and family antagonisms were a source of division in Florence. No sooner had the Ghibelline leaders finally fled from Florence in 1267 than the Guelfs themselves split into the two factions of Blacks and Whites. This led to fresh hatreds and bitterness, as well as to great sorrow for Dante, who was destined to spend the last twenty years of his life in exile. Reading the *Chronicles* of Giovanni Villani, a younger contemporary of Dante, one has the impression of Florence as a city almost continuously torn by feuds between Blacks and Whites, between family and family, between magnates and *popolani*.

Dante, poet and intellectual though he was, did not hold aloof from the affairs of his city. He seems to have fought against the Aretines in 1289 and was present at the siege of Caprona in the following year. Sometime before 1298 he married Gemma Donati, by whom he had at least four children, though virtually nothing else is known about his family life. In 1300 he went as Florentine ambassador to San Gimignano, and a few weeks later he was elected to serve as one of the six priors who were responsible for the affairs of the city for periods of two months. Florence was in a ferment; and during Dante's priorate it was decided to exile the leaders of both Blacks and Whites. Dante thereby had the sorrow of being instrumental in sending into exile his great friend, the poet Guido Cavalcanti, one of the leaders of the Whites. It was Cavalcanti who, feeling himself near death from malaria during his exile, wrote the ballad beginning 'Perch'io non spero di tornar giammai' (since I do not hope ever to return), which T.S. Eliot echoes at the beginning of 'Ash-Wednesday'. Dante was himself at this time a White Guelf, and in 1301 he was sent to Rome as a member of a White embassy to ask Pope Boniface VIII not to send Charles of Valois to Florence as a peacemaker. While he was still absent, however, Charles arrived in Florence and sided with the Blacks, who now gained control of the city. Dante, with other Whites, was condemned in his absence, first to fines and later to death. He never returned to Florence, and the rest of his life was spent in bitter exile. He seems to have wandered through most parts of northern Italy at various times. He was honourably received by the Scaligers of Verona and by Guido da Polenta at Ravenna, where he died in 1321.

Dante gives an account of one aspect of his youth in the *Vita Nuova*, his earliest book. He tells us that he first saw Beatrice when they were both in their ninth year, and that from that moment his heart was mastered by a great love for her. On the authority of his son Pietro and of Boccaccio, Beatrice is generally held to have been Bice, the daughter of Folco Portinari. Nine years later she greeted Dante in the street, a salutation which was the occasion of his earliest known sonnet. For the next few years this 'distant' love of Beatrice continued to be the inspiration of his poetry. Beatrice married Simone de' Bardi in 1287, but died in 1290. Dante was overwhelmed with grief at her death; and to console himself he turned to the study of philosophy. The *Vita Nuova* can seem a somewhat strange work to a modern reader. It has a threefold character: it is a narrative of the progress of Dante's love for Beatrice, an anthology of poems concerned with this love, and a literary analysis of these poems. The whole has a dream-like quality. The early poems are in the courtly love tradition, with a good deal of sighing and languishing. Then there comes a turning-point when the poet suddenly understands that his happiness can only lie in singing the praises of his lady in an objective manner. It is impossible to determine how much of the story of Dante's love for Beatrice is a literal account and how much may be a background for poetic invention; but there can surely be no doubt that he was inspired by the love of a real person. The turning-point I have mentioned is the beginning of the transfiguration of Beatrice. It is commonly held that Dante rewrote the last part of the book in later years, and it is in this last section that we read,

> There appeared to me a wonderful vision in which I saw things which made me decide to speak no more about that blessed one until I could do it more worthily. And that is why I am applying myself as much as I can, as she well knows; so that, if it please him by whom all things live to grant me a few more years, I hope to say of her what has never before been said of any woman.

It was in the *Divina Commedia* that Dante fulfilled the intention expressed in the last lines of the *Vita Nuova*. The whole of the *Commedia* was written during Dante's exile. It may have been begun about 1307, but he completed it only a few months before his death in 1321. Dante gave the poem the title *The Comedy*, because, as he explained, the poem has a sad beginning and a happy end, the epithet 'divine' being added in sixteenth-century printed editions. The 'story' of the poem is the narrative of Dante's imagined journey through the three realms beyond the grave, giving the three main divisions of *Inferno, Purgatorio* and *Paradiso*. Each *cantica* is itself divided into thirty-three cantos, and the *Inferno* has an introductory canto; so that there are one hundred in all, forming a poem of more than fourteen thousand lines with a strict rhyme scheme of Dante's own invention, called *terza rima*.

Dante imagines himself lost in a dark wood on Good Friday of the year 1300, when he was thirty-five years old 'in the middle of the journey of our life' (*Inferno* I i). There is a hill whose summit is bathed in sunlight, but the poet's way is barred by three fierce animals: a leopard, a lion and a she-wolf. To Dante in his terror there appears Virgil, who tells him that he has been sent by Beatrice to be Dante's guide. The two poets pass through the Gate of Hell with its inscription, whose grimness is well brought out by the heavy, ominous rhythm of the verse:

> Per me si va ne la città dolente,
> per me si va ne l'etterno dolore,
> per me si va tra la perduta gente. . . .
> Lasciate ogni speranza, voi ch'entrate
> (*Inferno* iii 1–3, 10)

*(Through me is the way into the sorrowful city; through me the way into eternal pain; through me the way amongst the lost people . . . Abandon all hope, you who enter)*

Dante imagines Hell as a series of nine decreasing circles descending to the centre of the earth. As he and Virgil pass through each circle they see the suffering of sinners of various types. The division of sins in the *Inferno* is roughly Aristotelian, with three main classes: sins of incontinence, of violence and of fraud. In the higher circles, for instance, he meets the sensualists and the avaricious; later on, murderers, suicides and usurers, and finally the worst sinners (in his eyes), those who have practised various kinds of fraud, from the seducers down to the traitors; and of all traitors the blackest are those who betray their benefactors. These last are with Satan in a lake of ice at the centre of the earth. Having passed through all the circles of Hell, Dante and Virgil find a path which leads them back to the surface of the earth antipodal to Jerusalem. Here at dawn on Easter Sunday they find themselves standing on the shores of an island from which there rises a high mountain, the Mount of Purgatory. A path circles round the mountain leading towards the summit, forming seven cornices, on each of which there are souls expiating their sins. The division here is the traditional Christian one of the seven capital sins; for example, the proud are found on the first cornice, whereas the slothful and the greedy are on higher slopes. Finally the pilgrims reach the summit where they find the Earthly Paradise. Virgil, the good pagan, the representative of unaided human reason, can go no further. He vanishes silently, his work completed. After a kind of mystical pageant of the Church, Beatrice appears, veiled at first. She upbraids Dante for a temporary unfaithfulness to herself and for his errors; and then, after he has been immersed in the waters of Lethe, she unveils herself and becomes his guide for the journey through the heavens of the *Paradiso*.

Dante uses the Ptolemaic astronomical system as the setting for the *Paradiso*. Each of seven concentric spheres contains a planet whose movement is regulated by the revolving of its sphere. Beyond these seven there lie the heaven of the fixed stars, then the Primum Mobile (from whose motion all else moves and beyond which there is neither space nor time) and finally the Empyrean. This last is Heaven in the true sense, where Dante the pilgrim will come to the vision of God. Many of the saints *appear* to Dante in the lower heavens, but their actual place of beatitude is in the Mystical Rose in the Empyrean. With Beatrice as his guide, Dante rises up through the successive heavens until he reaches the Empyrean. After Beatrice has left him to return to her place among the blessed, there comes the wonderful last canto of the poem, building up to the climax when Dante's intellect and will are finally caught up in God.

Dante in an earlier work, the *Convivio*, and in his letter to his patron in Verona, Can Grande della Scala, (if it is authentic) distinguishes between various layers of meaning in literary works, but he is not altogether consistent in the application of his classification. It is clear enough that the basic symbolic meaning of the poem is the consideration of the human race in general, and of Dante the pilgrim in particular, as a moral agent, and of what he makes of himself in the spiritual order by his use of free will in co-operating with or rejecting divine grace. Of allegory in the strict sense there is not a great deal in the *Divina Commedia*. It occurs occasionally, as in the three beasts of *Inferno* i; but in general Dante has a subtler method. For the most part he uses real human beings as his symbols, a method which gives much greater flexibility. Thus it would be wrong to see Virgil simply as a symbol of Natural Reason or Philosophy or Poetry; and Beatrice is not Theology or Grace or Divine Wisdom. The symbolism of real persons is complex since they themselves are complex beings. They symbolize what they are. So Virgil is a good pagan, wise and a poet, and Dante's literary master; Beatrice is one of the blessed in whom we see grace and a reflection of divine wisdom, and she is the woman Dante loved. Moreover they are individuals who have a personal relationship with Dante as a character in his poem. As regards Beatrice, this is obvious enough; but it is also true of Virgil. By the end of the arduous journey through the dark places of Hell and up the slopes of Purgatory there are deep ties of affection between Dante and his guide and teacher. This is brought out touchingly in *Purgatorio* xxx. Beatrice has just appeared, and although she is still veiled, Dante trembles all over as he feels 'old love's great power'. He turns for reassurance to Virgil; but Virgil is no longer there. Dante laments his loss with a triple pronouncement of the poet's name:

> Ma Virgilio n'avea lasciati scemi
> di sè, Virgilio dolcissimo patre,
> Virgilio a cui per mia salute die' mi.
>
> *Purgatorio* xxx 49–51

*(But Virgil had left us deprived of himself, Virgil dearest father, Virgil to whom I gave myself for my salvation.)*

What I have said of Dante's two guides is true of all those whom he meets on his journey. They are sinners or saints, each of whom is an example of what he symbolizes. Dante has peopled his poetic universe with real beings who are representatives of some particular aspect of evil or sanctity, but who are also individuals who interest us by their attitude towards their memory of life on earth and by their reaction to their present situation. They are not wooden abstractions as in so much medieval allegorical literature.

As I have said, the transfiguration of Beatrice had already begun in the latter part of the *Vita Nuova*. Dante's immediate predecessors and contemporaries in Tuscany had been changing the emphasis of the courtly love tradition of the Provençal poets and were expressing the idea of the ennobling influence which the mere sight and presence of their ladies could exert on the beholder. In the *Commedia* the mature Dante worked out this idea much more fully and daringly. He had great sensitivity to natural beauty and he saw every instance of created beauty as *splendore*, a reflection of divine beauty. Above all other such reflections was Beatrice; so Dante, at the memory of seeing her unveiled face at the summit of Purgatory, exclaims, 'O isplendor di viva luce etterna' ('O splendour of living eternal light': *Purgatorio* xxxi 139). On a number of occasions throughout the *Paradiso* Dante looks into her eyes and sees therein reflected the glory of Christ, the wisdom and beauty of God.

*

In the *Inferno* Dante uses the pictorial imagery of horrible physical sufferings and distortions to symbolize what human beings do to themselves by unrepented sin. At one point he turns to the reader and says, 'Do you think I could remain dry-faced when I saw our form so twisted . . . indeed I wept, leaning against a projection of the harsh rock' (*Inferno* xx 19–26). His descriptions of the horrors of Hell are powerful and vivid, perhaps especially the Wood of the Suicides in canto xiii, the horrible transformations of human forms into reptiles in canto xxv, and the traitors up to their chins in the frozen lake of the lowest circle, with their eternal tears eternally freezing on their eyelids. The *Inferno* provided subjects much more suited to Gustave Doré's talents as illustrator than did the other two *cantiche*.

The change in tone and atmosphere from the very beginning of the *Purgatorio* is remarkable. In the first canto there is a lyrical description of the changing colours of the dawn sky as Dante and Virgil arrive out of Hell onto the shores of Purgatory. There are, of course, descriptions of severe suffering; but it is suffering joyfully accepted as a necessary stage of purification on the way to God. The souls whom the pilgrims meet display humility, patience and fraternal love. The tone of the *cantica* is sometimes idyllic, sometimes evocative of the past. Some of the souls in Hell had expressed bitter remorse at their loss of the 'sweet earth'; but in Purgatory there is no more than a feeling of gentle melancholy in exile, as in this lovely passage with the exquisite cadence of its last line:

> Era già l'ora che volge il disio
> ai navicanti e'ntenerisce il core,
> lo dì c'han detto ai dolci amici addio,
> E che lo nova peregrin d'amore
> punge, se ode squilla di lontano
> che paia il giorno piange che si more . . .
>
> *Purgatorio* viii 1–6

*(It was now the hour that turns back the yearning of those who sail the seas and melts their hearts on the day that they have said farewell to dear friends, and pierces the new pilgrim with love if he hears from afar the bell that seems to mourn the dying day . . .)*

The *Purgatorio* is full of appreciation of beauty in nature and art, and there are the memories of youth, as Dante meets some of the poets and musicians of his younger days in Florence.

The *Paradiso* may have occasional longueurs but it remains an astonishing achievement. Few imaginative writers have treated successfully a theme of perfect happiness and fulfilment when all struggle is finished. Dante did not seek any easy way of portraying the complete happiness of the beatific vision. The souls whom he meets are not even clothed in human form; and such visual imagery as he uses is simply that of light. In the *Paradiso* he tries to express the double idea of the transcendence of God, to whom the blessed are united, and the immanence of God in his creation. However the theologians may argue, Dante clearly held that human beings had some sort of natural desire for God; and the supernatural end attained through *lumen gloriae* is the fulfilment of that desire. The whole *cantica* describes a journey towards that ultimate fulfilment, which is achieved in the final vision of the stupendous last canto. But Dante was above all a poet, a poet who saw the whole cosmos as a resemblance of its Creator. Throughout the *Paradiso* there is much use of the imagery of light, and of the reflection and refraction of light, to describe the reflected glory of the divine beauty. In the final vision he sees the whole of the created universe caught up by love in its Creator:

> Nel suo profondo vivi che s'interna,
> legato con amore in un volume,
> ciò che per l'universo si squaderna.
>
> *Paradiso* xxxiii 85–7

*(In the depth [of the eternal light] I saw that it contains, bound by love in one volume, that which is scattered like loose pages through the universe.)*

Of all created symbols which point towards the divine glory, Beatrice is for Dante the most potent. In her eyes and in her smile he is made aware of the light of eternal wisdom; and she grows ever more radiant as they rise together through the successive heavens, until even she no longer serves any purpose as a symbol of ultimate reality when the poet-pilgrim comes at last to the unveiled glory of the triune God. A word which recurs again and again in the *Paradiso* is *riso*, smile.

There is, of course, Beatrice's smile:

> Chè dentro alli occhi suoi ardea un riso
> tal ch'io pensai co'miei toccar lo fondo
> della mia grazia e del mio paradiso.
>
> *Paradiso* xv 34–6

*(For within her eyes there glowed such a smile that I thought I plumbed with mine the depths of my grace and of my paradise.)*

But for Dante the whole universe is smiling:

> Ciò ch'io vedeva mi sembiava un riso
> dell'universo.
>
> *Paradiso* xxvii 4–5

*(What I saw seemed to me a smile of the universe.)*

Every smile is a reflection of God's own smile in knowing and loving within the Trinity (cf. *Paradiso* xxxiii 124–6). *Riso* expresses joy, and Dante had written earlier: 'What is laughter but a scintillation of the soul's delight, a light showing outwardly an interior disposition?' (*Convivio* III viii 11)

*

The *Commedia* combines a wonderful unity of conception and symmetry of structure with the inspiration of individual incidents and a scrupulous care for detail. Dante was familiar with an amazingly wide area of what was then the sum of human knowledge, his work abounding in detailed allusions to Scripture, theology, philosophy, literature, astronomy, geography, history and politics. This is the more astonishing when one remembers that he lived before the era of printed books. None of this wide range of knowledge, however, appears as miscellaneous information; all is transmuted by Dante to become part of his poetic creation. One wonders how, on the one hand, he would have absorbed and used modern knowledge of, say, relativity, sub-atomic physics, logic and the subconscious, and how, on the other hand, his fierce indignation might have been roused to achieve great poetry by admass culture, expense accounts and the glamorizing of the trivial and the sordid.

Dante had the poet's sharp eye for detailed observation. No preoccupation with the 'grand style' inhibited him from using for the most part similes drawn from everyday things, such as are to be seen in the countryside or kitchen. Here is his description of himself at one point when he is eager to ask Virgil for an explanation but is too diffident to speak out:

> E quale il cicognin che leva l'ala
> per voglia di volare, e non s'attenta
> d'abbondonar lo nido, e giù la cala;
> Tal era io . . .

*Purgatorio* xxv 10–13

*(And like a baby stork that lifts its wing with a longing to fly and, not daring to leave the nest, drops it again; So was I . . .)*

Although he is taking us on a journey through other worlds, Dante continually refers us back to earthly life. So, for example, when he is describing the horror of seeing sinners up to their necks in the frozen lake of the lowest circle of Hell, he adds an aside that even now he shudders when he sees a frozen pool (*Inferno* xxxii 71–2).

The human beings whose spirits Dante meets on his journey are for us remote historical figures, so that we are apt to forget that many of them were contemporaries or near contemporaries, some indeed friends or enemies of the poet. It is as though a writer of today were to commit himself to a judgement on the eternal destiny of many famous public figures of the last few decades – politicians, ecclesiastics, writers – as well as some family acquaintances. His treatment of individuals is extremely skilful. The situation in the *Commedia* is static, not dynamic. The poet could not show any development of character, since the earthly lives of all his personages are over and their fates eternally fixed. He makes them interesting to the reader by the drama of their memories and by their reactions to divine justice. They are individuals in a world, but it is a world beyond the tomb.

*

Dante's political views are an important strand in his thought and poetry. In a Latin work, *De Monarchia*, he developed his ideas for a single universal monarch to ensure the peace and justice that people require to be able to lead happy lives, and – well ahead of his time – he argued for the independence of the respective powers of Church and State. It is also worth mentioning Dante's ambivalent attitude towards his native city. In the letter to Can Grande, if it was he who wrote it, he describes himself as 'Florentinus natione sed non moribus', a Florentine by birth but not by character. He had a passion for justice – in another letter he describes himself as 'a man preaching justice' – and he saw Florence as monstrously unjust, both in its treatment of himself and in its politics. He applies to it abusive terms, such as 'nest of malice' (*Inferno* xv 78); and there are a number of fierce denunciations of Florence scattered throughout the poem, even in the *Paradiso*, the most bitterly ironic coming in a triple antithesis when Dante the pilgrim is on the very threshold of the divine vision:

> Ïo, che al divino dall'umano,
> all'etterno dal tempo era venuto,
> e di Fiorenza in popol giusto e sano . . .
>
> *Paradiso* xxxi 37–9

*(I who had come to the divine from the human, to the eternal from time, and from Florence to a just and upright people . . .)*

But he felt so passionately only because he loved Florence so much, 'the lovely sheepfold where I slept as a lamb' (*Paradiso* xxv 5); and there is a moving passage in the *Convivio*, written in the earlier years of his exile:

> It was the pleasure of the citizens of Florence, the fairest and most famous daughter of Rome, to cast me out of her sweet bosom, in which I was born and brought to the summit of life, and in which I long with all my heart to rest my weary spirit and to end my allotted time.
>
> (*Convivio* I iii)

*

In the lines quoted at the beginning of the chapter, it is characteristic of Dante that, even as he approached the sublime climax of the *Paradiso*, he should use the word *donnea*, a word of Provençal origin from the troubadour tradition with connotations of amorous dalliance. He burned with desire to look again at Beatrice, who was not only the woman he loved but also the living symbol of Christian wisdom. His mind in love was passionate in its search for knowledge and truth.

In one of the most wonderful episodes in the *Inferno*, Dante the character meets Ulysses in the circle of the deceitful (canto xxvi), where he is being punished for his cunning and trickery in the stratagem of the wooden horse which led to the fall of Troy. Ulysses recounts his last and fatal journey, when, as an old man with a few faithful companions, he sailed through the Straits of Gibraltar and down into the southern hemisphere (unexplored in Dante's time) where their ship foundered in a storm, and they were all drowned. Ulysses says that he was driven by a passion to gain knowledge of the world, and he repeats the speech which he made to his men before they set out, urging that, in the short time that remained to them, they should not deny experience, ending with the tremendous flourish of

> Considerate la vostra semenza:
> fatti non foste a viver come bruti,
> ma per seguir virtute e conoscenza.
>
> *Inferno* xxvi 118–20

*(Think of the breed from which you spring. You were not born to live like brutes, but to follow after human worth and knowledge.)*

As on many other occasions, the poet achieves dramatic tension by eliciting our admiration for one side of a sinner's character while leaving him to suffer for his unrepented wickedness. In this instance, Dante surely saw something of himself in Ulysses' passion for knowledge and for experience.

Dante, however, was not concerned merely with the thirst for factual knowledge or even for life experience. As I have mentioned, he says in the *Vita Nuova* that he turned to the study of philosophy to console himself after Beatrice's death. One can truly say that he proceeded to 'fall in love' with philosophy. The *Convivio*, which he wrote between the *Vita Nuova* and the *Commedia*, and which he left unfinished, consists of long commentaries on three *canzoni* (there were to have been fourteen). The extraordinary thing about two of these poems is that they are praise-lyrics to his lady in the same style and language that he had used in the later poems of the *Vita Nuova* – but the 'lady' is now philosophy. Both in the poems and in the commentaries, Dante speaks of yearning to look on his lady, of the beauty of her eyes and of her smile, and so on. His longing to seek and to contemplate truth, his passionate enthusiasm for intellectual activity come through to us in these allegorical poems. During their journey together through the ten heavens of the *Paradiso*, Beatrice several times applauds Dante's questions, because they show his desire to seek the truth that leads to wisdom.

# 5

# The Way to the Centre

La donna mia, che mi vedea in cura
forte sospeso, disse: 'Da quel punto
depende il cielo e tutto la natura'

*Paradiso* xxviii 40–2

*(My lady, who saw me expectant and uncertain, said: 'From that point hang the heavens and all nature')*

THREE TIMES IN THE last cantos of the *Inferno* (xxxii 2–3, 73, xxxiv 111) Dante refers to the force of gravity which draws everything towards the centre of the earth, where it was thought that gravity was strongest. He makes us feel the weight of evil pressing down more and more as we approach the place where Satan lies. In the Ptolemaic astronomical system the earth was at the centre of the universe, with the planets and the stars revolving around it; so in a sense it seems, as we read, that Evil is at the very centre of the whole of creation.

The memory of this sense of oppression grows fainter as we accompany Dante up the Mount of Purgatory and through the heavens of the *Paradiso*; but it is not until Canto 28 of the *Paradiso* that the impression is shown to have been false. Dante is gazing into Beatrice's eyes ('the beautiful eyes from which Love made the cord to catch me' [11–12]) when he sees a light reflected in them. He turns around to find the source of this reflection, and sees an intensely bright point of light, so small that 'the smallest star would look like a moon beside it'

(19–20). Beatrice explains that this is a vision of God, a symbolic vision of God, not yet the real beatific vision in which his intellect and will are finally going to be caught up as described in the last lines of the poem. Dante sees nine fiery concentric circles wheeling around this brilliant point of light which symbolizes God. These are the paths of the traditional nine 'orders' of angels. The highest, the Seraphim, move around the circle of smallest radius. Then come the Cherubim, and so on down to the Angels whose circle has the largest radius. Now in Dante's journey through the material heavens the order was exactly the opposite: the Angels were the 'moving intelligences' of the Moon, the lowest heaven, whose orbit around the earth was the smallest, while the Seraphim were the movers of the sphere of the ninth heaven, the most remote from earth.

Suddenly we realize that everything has been turned inside out. Materially, the earth is at the centre with the heavens circling round it, and at the centre of the earth lies Satan and the power of evil. Now we see that this is not the ultimate reality. On the contrary, at the centre of reality is God, on whom all else depends. All creatures move around him, held on their courses by centripetal force, with the highest creatures moving in the narrowest circle because of their greater love for God. And who is this God, on whom all else depends? Not Aristotle's impersonal unmoved Mover, but 'the Love which moves the sun and the other stars', as Dante will say in the very last line of the poem.

The deepest unifying element in the *Commedia* is to be found in the theme of love, human and divine. Human love can 'go wrong', it is redeemable, and finally it can reach total union with divine love. Three episodes illustrate this, one from each of the *cantiche*. First, what has probably been the most famous episode in the *Comedy* since the days of the nineteenth-century Romantics: the story of Paolo and Francesca in *Inferno* v. Dante and Virgil have just descended into the second circle, where they see a multitude of spirits, weeping and lamenting as they are whirled endlessly around by a fierce wind. These are the lustful who have died unrepentant. At Dante's request, two who are being blown about together on the blast speak to him. It is Francesca who tells how Paolo, her husband's brother, had become her lover, and how her husband, taking them by surprise, had killed them both. Francesca da Polenta was married to Gianciotto Malatesta, Lord of Rimini, whose younger brother Dante must have known at least by sight when he was Capitano del Popolo in Florence in 1282; and it was Francesca's nephew, Guido Novello, who was Dante's host during the last years of his life in Ravenna. Contemporary chroniclers make no mention of the double murder, but Dante's son, Pietro, in his commentary takes it as a well-known fact, which must have occurred in about 1285.

Dante presents the story with consummate skill. Francesca explains that she was unable to resist reciprocating Paolo's love. One day they were reading together the story of Lancelot's adulterous love for Guinevere in the Arthurian legend:

> Quando legemmo il disiato riso
>     esser baciato da cotanto amante,
>     questi, che mai da me non fia diviso,
> la bocca mi baciò tutto tremante.
>     Galeotto fu il libro e chi lo scrisse:
>     quel giorno più non vi leggemmo avante.

*(When we read that the desired smile was kissed by so great a lover, he who will never be parted from me, all trembling, kissed my mouth. A Galehalt [pander] was the book and he that wrote it. That day we read no more of it.)*

We might be tempted, like nineteenth-century Romantic critics, to consider Francesca a sort of tragic heroine; but that would be to misunderstand the poet's intentions. Francesca tells her sad story in the most poignant verse, and at the end Dante faints out of sheer human pity. We must remember, however, that for him the tragedy was not that their disordered love had led to death, but that, unrepented, it had warped them as human beings for all eternity. The Paolo and Francesca episode is a supreme example of Dante's ability to hold in tension his human sympathy and the undeviating realism of his moral beliefs. The *pietade* which overcomes him, as a character, on hearing Francesca's story is not just pity in the modern sense; it is a compassion that includes a certain trouble of mind in the listener at the thought that he could be capable of the same sin. We must never forget that, as Virgil told him at the very beginning of the poem, Dante, the representative of Everyman, is to be guided through the realms beyond the grave as a moral education leading to wisdom. 'A Galehalt was the book and he that wrote it' – one line evokes the whole spirit of chivalric romance and the dangerous falseness that always lurked within it.

For the second episode we move to the last and highest terrace on the Mount of Purgatory, where Dante meets spirits who are being purified from the effects of their repented sexual sins (Canto 26). He sees some of them moving within a wall of fire and then two groups going rapidly in opposite directions. As they pass each other they give a brief reciprocal kiss of greeting. Dante compares their action to that of a swarm of ants moving in different directions and nuzzling each other rapidly 'perhaps to ask the way or the news'. This quick kiss of affection of the repentant carnal sinners is in contrast to the lingering kiss of Paolo and Francesca. One shade who comes close to Dante, though making sure of remaining in the refining fire, reveals himself as Guido Guinizelli. Dante is deeply affected:

> . . . Quand' io odo nomar sè stesso il padre
> mio e delli altri miei miglior che mai

rime d'amore usar dolci e leggiadre

*Purgatorio* xxvi 97–9

*(When I hear him name himself, [who is] the father of me and of others my betters, who have ever used sweet and graceful verses of love)*

A generation older than Dante, Guinizelli was a Bolognese who gave the lead in breaking away from the arid style of earlier Italian poets, a lead which was to inspire Dante to achieve in his lyric poetry the 'sweet new style', *lo dolce stil novo*, as he himself makes Bonagiunta da Lucca call it in *Purgatorio* xxiv. Guinizelli and Dante talk about poets and poetic technique; but behind that lies Dante the writer's moral purpose in this canto. *Amor de lonh*, of troubadour tradition, did not by any means always remain 'love at a distance'; and Guinizelli explains that the repentant lustful are being purified on this terrace 'because we did not observe human law, following appetite like beasts'. As always, Dante is here emphasizing that all sin is a distorting of what rational human nature ought to be.

This links up with our third episode beginning with the opening of *Paradiso* viii:

Solea creder lo mondo in suo periclo
che la bella Ciprigna il folle amore
raggiasse . . .

*Paradiso* viii 1–3

*(The world used to believe, to its peril, that the beautiful Cyprian [i.e. Venus] flashed forth mad love . . .)*

Dante and Beatrice have just risen to the third heaven, that of Venus. The poet begins by saying that in the ancient world the influence of Venus was held to be irresistible and love a kind of madness beyond the control of reason. (Not unlike romantic fiction's 'This thing is bigger than both of us'.) The lyric poets preceding Dante – and he himself in his early poems – also often imply that love takes hold of the heart in an irresistible way. In the *Comedy* he is at pains to correct this view; for instance, by making Francesca imply it in her emphatic placing of *amor* at the beginning of three successive tercets:

Amor, ch'al cor gentil ratto s'apprende . . .
Amor, ch'a nullo amato amar perdona . . .
Amor, condusse noi ad una morte.

*Inferno* v 100,103,106

*(Love which quickly takes hold of the gentle heart . . . Love which does not permit any loved one not to love . . . Love brought us to one death.)*

In *Paradiso* viii and ix, he is concerned with the matter of temperament which inclines us to act in one way rather than another. As he insists, this does not take away free will nor absolve us from responsibility for our actions. In this Heaven of Venus he meets Cunizza, an amorous lady from Northern Italy, who had several husbands and more lovers. In her old age she lived in Florence as a guest of the Cavalcanti family and had a reputation for a loving compassion towards the unfortunate. Dante was fifteen when she died, and he must surely have known of her from his Cavalcanti friends, even if he did not meet her. In the poem she introduces herself:

Cunizza fui chiamata, e qui refulgo
  perché mi vinse il lume d'esta stella;
ma lietamente a me medesma indulgo
  la cagion di mia sorte, e non mi noia.

*Paradiso* ix 32–5

*(I was called Cunizza, and I shine here because the light of this*

*star [Venus] overcame me; but I joyfully forgive myself the cause of my destiny, and it does not grieve me.)*

She rejoices that it was precisely *through* her affectionate temperament, rightly used in the end, that she achieved her blissful destiny.

The other spirit who speaks to Dante in this heaven is Folquetz of Marseilles, a troubadour poet who later became a Cistercian monk and Abbot of Le Thoronet. (Dante passes over the fact that, in his later life as Bishop of Toulouse, he was a merciless persecutor of Albigensian heretics.) He tells Dante that he and his companions smile, not because of their faults, from which they have been purified, but because their affectionate temperament is a reflection of the love by which God governs his creation.

*

A moving example from our century of Dante's point that a passionate temperament may be the very means of bringing a person to sanctity and union with God is provided by Etty Hillesum, a Dutch Jewess who died in Auschwitz in late 1943.

Not much is known of her life before the eighteen months covered by her diaries, which she began in March 1941 at the age of twenty-seven and kept during the horrors of the Nazi occupation of Holland and with the growing certainty of her own ultimate fate.

She had a number of lovers, and the first entry in her diary reads: 'I am accomplished in bed . . . love does indeed suit me to perfection, and yet it remains a mere trifle, set apart from what is truly essential, and deep inside me something is still locked away.' Eight months later she writes:

> . . . I walk down the street next to a man and look up at him radiantly. Yet just twelve hours ago I lay in the arms

> of another man and loved him then and love him now. Is this decadent? To me it feels perfectly all right. Perhaps because the physical thing is no longer so essential to me. The love I now feel is different, wider. Am I fooling myself? I don't think so.

It was through her relationship with an unusual older man, Julius Spier, that she began her journey to God. After his death in 1942, she wrote: 'You were the mediator between me and God, and now you, the mediator, have gone and my path leads straight to God. It is right that it should be so. And I shall be the mediator for any soul I can reach.' Amid the growing darkness of external events, Etty Hillesum developed a contemplative's love of God, overflowing into an unconditional love for all her fellow humans. At the beginning of this development she wrote:

> God, take me by the hand, I shall follow you dutifully, and not resist too much. I shall evade none of the tempests life has in store for me . . . I shall follow you wherever your hand leads me and shall try not to be afraid . . . I shall try to spread some of my warmth, of my love for others. But we shouldn't boast of our love for others. We cannot be sure it really exists.

A few months later she was able to write:

> Once you have begun to walk with God, you need only keep on walking with him and all life becomes one long stroll . . . I hate nobody. I am not embittered. Once the love of mankind has germinated in you, it will grow without measure.

She faced her own self with relentless honesty and her approaching end with fear and immense courage: 'I have looked our destruction, our miserable end which has already begun, straight in the eye and accepted it into my life, and my love has not been diminished . . . By excluding death from our life we cannot live a full life, and by admitting death into our life we enlarge and enrich it.'

Etty volunteered to accompany the first set of Jews sent to Westerbork camp, the transit camp for Auschwitz. Among the last entries in her diaries we read: 'At night, as I lay on my plank bed, surrounded by women and girls, gently snoring, dreaming aloud, quietly sobbing and tossing and turning, I was sometimes filled with an infinite tenderness . . . and I prayed "Let me be the thinking heart of these barracks". And that is what I want to be again.' And the next day: 'Alone for once in the middle of the night. God and I have been left together, and I feel all the richer and at peace for it.' Finally, the very last entry: 'We should be willing to act as a balm for all wounds.'

The whole diary, covering only eighteen months, forms a moving record of the transforming power of love.

*

I have looked at examples of sexual love, either disordered or being purified or having finally brought an individual to union with divine love. Dante in fact saw love as the energizer of *all* human action.

The poet has Virgil expound this in Scholastic philosophical terms in Cantos 17 and 18 of the *Purgatorio.* Night is falling on Mount Purgatory and Dante can climb no further after sunset (because purgation is only possible in the light of grace). To make good use of the enforced halt, Virgil gives Dante a discourse on love. His immediate purpose is to explain why certain classes of penitent sinners are on the various terraces of the mountain; but his discourse is of far wider significance for an understanding of the whole poem.

In the preceding canto, one of the spirits had explained to Dante in a lovely passage (which inspired T.S. Eliot's 'Animula') that from their moment of birth human beings, because they come from a loving God, desire what pleases:

> Esce di mano a lui che la vagheggia
>   prima che sia, a guisa di fanciulla
>   che piangendo e ridendo pargoleggia,
> l'anima semplicetta che sa nulla,
>   salvo che, mosso da lieto fattore,
>   volentier torna a ciò che la trastulla.
>
> *Purgatorio* xvi 85–90

*(From the hand of him who regards it lovingly before it exists, there comes forth, like a child that plays, weeping and smiling, the little simple soul that knows nothing, but, moved by its joyful Maker, turns with desire to what delights it.)*

> 'Né creator né creatura mai'
>   cominciò el 'figliuol, fu senza amore,
>   o naturale o d'animo . . .'.
>
> *Purgatorio* xvii 91–3

*('Neither creator nor creature, my son,' he began 'was ever without love, either natural or rational . . .'.)*

So begins Virgil's discourse on love. By 'natural love' the Scholastics meant that every being has a 'desire', i.e. a tendency, towards the fulfilment appropriate to its nature. Beings endowed with intellect have, in addition, a 'rational love'. Virgil now says that, whereas 'natural love' cannot err since it comes from the very nature of the being created by God, the other love *can* go wrong because rational creatures have the power of choice. They may choose to love a wrong object or a right object badly (too much or too little). Then comes the assertion that is most important for our present consideration: 'From this you can understand that love must be the seed in you of every virtue and of every action which deserves punishment' (103–5).

So the spring of all human activity is love, and all morality a matter of what a person loves and how he or she loves.

Virgil then explains the divisions of Purgatory in terms of the various possible perversions of human love and of its excesses and defects. The details are not relevant here; but he makes one other very important point. He says that all human beings have a 'confused apprehension' of a good in which they may hope to rest. In other words, everyone seeks happiness; and he adds that ultimately this can only be found in God who is 'the fruit and root of every good' (135). The whole of the *Paradiso* will be concerned with the journey to this fulfilment. We have here an echo of St Augustine: 'You have made us for yourself, and our hearts are restless until they rest in you' (*Confessions* I).

In Canto 18 Virgil explains that there are three stages in every moral act. First, we apprehend an external reality, to which (secondly), if it pleases us, we are naturally attracted. Finally, our will consents to go out to the object and enjoys it. We have no control over the first two stages; it is the third stage that is crucial. Love is not always good: the morality of the act depends on a correct judgement. Virgil says that we have a power that enables us to control the desire which arises naturally in us. This 'noble faculty' is free will.

To round off two rather abstract cantos, Dante had a brilliant idea, perhaps a little clumsy in its execution. He says that, when Virgil had finished speaking, he, Dante, slipped into sleep and dreamed that he saw an ugly, deformed woman; but as he looked at her, his gaze itself made her beautiful 'as love desires'. She called herself the 'Sweet Siren who bewitches'; but Virgil appeared in the dream, and revealed her true loathsomeness. Here we have the subjective process by which human beings persuade themselves of the desirability of some evil. The siren is the false Beatrice.

As he descends the nine circles of Hell, Dante sees human

nature becoming progressively distorted as love becomes more and more perverted. In the upper circles, sins of intemperance are punished, sins arising from real but disordered love of *true* goods: sex, comfortable living, possessions. Lower down are found those whose evil deeds have involved damage to others through violence or some form of malice, which, Virgil says, 'destroys the bond of love'. Near the beginning of his journey through Hell, Dante had seen the forms of Paolo and Francesca still united in love, though a love that now brought them eternal suffering. By the time he reached the lowest circle he found this mutuality had turned into bitter hatred:

> . . . io vidi due ghiacciati in una buca,
> sì che l'un capo all'altro era cappello;
> e come 'l pan per fame si manduca,
> così 'l sovran li denti all'altro pose
> la 've 'l cervel s'aggiunge con la nuca.
>
> (*Inferno* xxxii 125–9)

*(I saw two frozen in one hole so that one head was a hood to the other; and, as bread is eaten for hunger, so the one on top set his teeth in the other one where the brain joins the back of the neck.)*

These are the heads of Archbishop Ruggieri and Count Ugolino. During a power struggle in Pisa in 1289 the Archbishop had treacherously imprisoned Count Ugolino (who himself was a betrayer of others) and left him with two sons and two grandsons to die of starvation. Before beginning to tell his story, Ugolino 'lifted his mouth from the savage meal, cleaning it on the hair of the head he had wasted at the back'. Once again the poet creates dramatic tension, arousing our sympathy for an evil man by the pathos of Ugolino's account of the days of agony endured by himself and his family after they had heard the door of the tower being nailed up.

*

In the *Inferno* we see human love 'gone wrong' and in the *Purgatorio* the 'putting right' of love. The *Paradiso* is concerned with the journey of human love to its final end, union with the Divine Love which is the centre of all reality. Immediately in Canto 1 Beatrice takes up in theological terms Virgil's philosophical explanation that all beings have inborn tendencies which lead them to the fulfilment of their natures. All creatures, Beatrice says, bear the impress of their Creator and, according to their natures, 'they move to different ports through the great sea of being' (112–13). This is true also of beings with intellect and will; and so, she explains to Dante, the two of them are now being borne towards the place of perfect human fulfilment 'by the power of the bowstring which aims the arrow at a joyful mark'. That image describing the concentrated energy of the purified desire for union with God is typical of Dante.

At the beginning of the canto, the poet speaks of 'our intellect approaching its desire'. For Dante the innate desire for God is a desire to know as well as to love. In his time there were two schools of thought about what constituted the *essence* of beatitude: knowledge or love. Broadly speaking, the Dominican theologians maintained the former, and the Franciscans the latter. Dante, despite his sympathy with the Franciscan spirit, comes down firmly on the Dominican side in this matter. He makes Beatrice say of the blessed:

> E dei saper che tutti hanno diletto
> quanto la sua veduta si profonda
> nel vero in che si queta ogni intelletto.
> Quinci si può veder come si fonda
> l'esser beato nell'atto che vede,
> non in quel ch'ama, che poscia seconda.
>
> *Paradiso* xxviii 106–11

*(And you must know that all have delight according to the depth to which their sight penetrates into the truth in which every intellect*

*finds rest. Whence it may be seen how blessedness is founded in the act of vision, not in that of love, which follows after.)*

Surely it can be said that in this life, while it is true that love is consequent upon knowledge, it is equally true that we cannot know deeply until we have learned to love. Dante's desire to know truth was as passionate as his love. Moreover, he always sees error as the root of sin. As soon as he and Virgil have passed through the gates of Hell, Virgil explains that they have come to the place where

> . . . tu vedrai le genti dolorose,
> c'hanno perduto il ben de l'intelletto.
>
> *Inferno* iii 17–18

*( . . . You will see the sorrowful people who have lost the good of the intellect [i.e. the Truth which is God].)*

The *Paradiso* is a journey to the Truth, giving delight to the will. Frequently during this journey Dante seeks knowledge by questioning Beatrice, always to her joy; for instance, after one such query,

> Beatrice mi guardò con li occhi pieni
> di faville d'amor così divini,
> che, vinta, mia virtute diè le reni,
> e quasi mi perdei con li occhi chini.
>
> *Paradiso* iv 139–42

*(Beatrice looked at me with eyes so divine and full of such sparkling of love that, overcome, my power fled, and with downcast eyes I was almost lost.)*

Before reaching his ultimate vision, Dante has to undergo 'examinations' on faith, hope and love, carried out by St Peter, St James and St John. It is appropriate that John should be the examiner in love since in his First Letter he proclaimed that God is love and went on to analyze what should be our response to God's gratuitous love for us (1 John 4). In Canto 26 he begins by asking the 'candidate' what is the object of his love. Dante replies that God is the ultimate object of all his love. Asked to expand this reply, he says that it is goodness which enkindles love, and that all created goodness is simply a reflection of the Divine Goodness. He says that he knows this both by reason and by revelation. St John continues, 'the highest of your loves looks to God, but say further whether you feel any other cords drawing you towards him' (48–50). This elicits a magnificent response from Dante, who replies that everything that can make the heart turn to God – the world, his own existence, the saving death of Christ – all of them

tratto m'hanno del mar dell'amor torto,
e del diritto m'han posto alla riva.
Le fronde onde s'infronda tutto l'orto
dell'ortolano etterno, am' io cotanto
quanto da lui a lor di bene è porto.

*Paradiso* xxvi 62–6

*(have drawn me from the sea of twisted love and have brought me to the shore of right love. The leaves with which all the garden of the eternal gardener is enleafed I love to the extent of the good that they have received from him.)*

This is the most detailed statement of Dante's appreciation of the goodness and beauty of the created world as a participation in God's infinite goodness and beauty. It expands what he wrote in the first tercet of the *Paradiso*, with its majestic opening line:

La gloria di colui che tutto move
per l'universo penetra e risplende
in una parte più e meno altrove

*Paradiso* i 1–3

*(The glory of him who moves all things penetrates the universe and shines more in one part and less in another)*

All through the poem his similes show his close observation of nature and his delight in the material world. The beauty of the starry heavens held a particular attraction for him; and in one daring image the poet compares himself to a falcon with God as the falconer using the wheeling heavens as a lure to attract his creature (*Purgatorio* xix 62–7).

In all this Dante is following the traditional medieval way of thought in which God's revelation was seen as coming to humans in two books: the Book of Scripture and the Book of Nature. Every created thing was *vestigium Dei*, a 'trace' of God. Human beings, of course, by virtue of their intellect and will, bore a much closer resemblance to God as *imago Dei*, referring back to Genesis 1:27: 'God created man in the image of himself, in the image of God he created him, male and female he created them.'

We need to remember that for Dante human love was above all concerned with truth and virtue, as he himself says in the Commentary in the *Convivio* on his *canzone*, beginning *Amor che ne la mente mi ragiona* ('Love which speaks to me in my mind'). Later in that poem he writes of 'the lady of whom Love makes me speak'. The lady is philosophy, understood in its original sense as knowledge of the truth which leads to moral goodness and hence to wisdom. We are not used to these matters being treated in such a lyrical manner; but this *canzone* appears again at another lyrical moment, this time in the *Comedy* itself. As Dante arrives on the shores of Purgatory, his eyes are gladdened by the lovely colours of dawn 'as soon as I came out from the dead air which had oppressed my eyes and breast', and he can see afar the shimmering of the sea in the early morning light. From among a group of penitent souls one comes forward with a gesture of affection. This is Casella, a Florentine musician who had set some of Dante's poems to music. Dante asks him to sing one of 'the love songs which used to quieten all my desires'.

> 'Amor che ne la mente mi ragiona'
> Comminciò elli allor sì dolcemente,
> Che la dolcezza ancor dentro mi sona.
>
> *Purgatorio* ii 112–14

*('Love which speaks to me in my mind', he then began so sweetly that the sweetness still sounds within me.)*

Dante, Virgil and all those penitent spirits listen with rapt attention to Casella's song.

Love, beauty, truth, virtue, wisdom: all are interwoven in Dante's mind and in his poetry. As he gazes on Beatrice's beauty in the *Paradiso*, he is gazing on the transfigured woman whom he had loved on earth, and at the same time he is gazing in contemplation on an image of divine truth, goodness and love. In his last words of gratitude to Beatrice when she has left him to return to her place in the Empyrean he says:

> Tu m'hai di servo tratto a libertate
>
> *Paradiso* xxxi 85

*(You have drawn me from being a slave [of error] into freedom [of truth])*

*

Beatrice has left Dante because ultimately no created reflection of God can fully satisfy human thirst for fulfilment of mind and heart. In the last canto of the *Paradiso* all created images are finally left behind. The poet imagines himself approaching, and finally reaching, the end of his journey to the centre of reality, which is at the same time the goal of human longing ('I, who was approaching the end of all desires' xxxiii 46–7). He says: 'Henceforward my vision was greater than our speech . . . and memory fails at such excess' (53–7). With a subtle appeal to our experience of dreams, he goes on:

Qual è colui che somnïando vede,
  che dopo il sogno la passione impressa
  rimane, e l'altro alla mente non riede,
Cotal son io, chè quasi tutta cessa
  mia visïone, ed ancor mi distilla
  nel core il dolce che nacque da essa.
Così la neve al sol si disigilla;

*Paradiso* xxxiii 58–64

*(Like one who sees in a dream, and after the dream the feeling roused by it remains and the rest does not return to the mind, so am I; for my vision almost totally fades away, and still there drops into my heart the sweetness born of it. So the snow dissolves in the sun.)*

This is the first of several occasions in the last hundred lines of the poem in which Dante refers to a kind of 'double ineffability'. An experience may be inexpressible, first because words are inadequate, secondly – and more profoundly – because thought itself is incapable of comprehending it. This idea had been with Dante at least since the period when he was writing the *Convivio*. As I said at the end of the Introduction to this book, poetry can often come nearest to expressing the inexpressible; but there are further depths, not only beyond words, but beyond concepts.

In this final canto the poet is, of course, *imagining* himself coming to the ultimate ineffable experience. When he speaks (as a character) of his memory failing him in the attempt to express his experience, he does not mean that he had forgotten it, but that it is impossible to conceptualize its reality. Before reaching full union with God, Dante has three symbolic visions. First, in lines which I have already quoted in Chapter 4, he describes a vision of the whole of creation in all its variety caught up into a unity by its Creator's love. Then he has two further visions *representing* the Trinity and the incarnation, and again exclaims how inadequate speech is to express his concept of what he saw and how weak the concept itself compared with the reality. Now at last Dante, the pilgrim who has been guided through the realms of human evil, of repentance and of holiness, is ready to experience the reality of ultimate human fulfilment:

All' alta fantasia qui mancò possa;
  Ma già volgeva il mio disio e'l velle,
  sì come rota ch' igualmente è mossa,
l'amor che move il sole e l'altre stelle.

*Paradiso* xxxiii 142–5

*(Here power failed the high phantasy [concept-forming faculty]; but now my desire and will, like a wheel that moves perfectly smoothly, were being turned by the love that moves the sun and the other stars.)*

Now the human will was moving in the perfect freedom of mutual love with its Creator. One perennial difficulty in discourse about God, whether theological or devotional, is that it is almost impossible to avoid speaking as though God were an object among other objects, one being over against other beings, no matter what qualifications we may make. Dante astonishingly succeeded in avoiding this by speaking simply in terms of relationship.

I find it deeply moving to witness the transformation of the young Dante of the early part of the *Vita Nuova* 'in love with love' (as St Augustine describes his own adolescent self) into the supreme poet whose experience of life – much of it bitter – combined with intense intellectual activity, had brought him to understand that love was at the centre of all reality. But Dante himself would not have been satisfied for us just to admire 'il poema sacro / al quale ha posto mano e cielo e terra' (*Paradiso* xxv 1–2: the sacred poem / to which heaven and earth have set their hand, i.e. his poem inspired both by Christian faith and by experience of life on earth). During the course of his pilgrim's journey, he frequently reminds us that he is writing for his reader's instruction, whether he is describing the horrible effects of evil on the human person or the sublimity of union with the Love that moves the universe. He wanted us to consider and to grow wise.

# 6

# The Old Man of Crete

O cry created as the bow of sin
Is drawn across our trembling violin.
*O weep, child, weep, O weep away the stain.*
W.H. Auden: 'Anthem for St Cecilia's Day'

THERE IS A STRANGELY moving incident in *Inferno* Canto 14. Strange for two reasons: first, because it occurs in an apparently prosaic passage in which Virgil is simply explaining to Dante a detail about the topography of Hell, and, secondly, because the lines themselves are concerned with an allegorical figure not much to the modern taste.

Dante and Virgil have just emerged from the Wood of Suicides, where they have heard Pier della Vigna's poignant account of how he had taken his own life after he had been blinded and imprisoned because of false accusations of treachery against the Emperor Frederick II, to whom, he insists, he had in fact always been loyal. Coming out of the wood, the two poets see a plain of burning sand, on which a crowd of naked sinners are tormented under a rain of fire-flakes. The scene evokes a sense of barrenness; and the sins punished here do indeed have a common characteristic of sterility, although we may at first be somewhat surprised by their juxtaposition: blasphemy, sodomy and usury – that is, sins of 'violence' against God, nature and art (in the sense of human industry). The grouping of these three sins together is due perhaps to a particularly medieval way of thinking. It was one of the early commentators on the *Divina Commedia* who remarked that, while sodomy made sterile what should be fertile, usury perversely rendered fertile what is of its nature sterile.

After they have heard one of the blasphemers, Capaneus, railing against Heaven, and Virgil has rebuked him with 'no torment other than your own rage would be suffering to match your fury', Dante and his guide come to a stream whose blood-red colour 'makes me shudder even now'. Virgil begins his explanation of its significance and place in the arrangement of Hell by describing *un gran veglio*, 'a great old man', who stands on the island of Crete. His head is of gold, his breast and arms of silver, the rest of his trunk of brass, his legs and feet of iron, except his right foot which is of clay. This description comes straight from the Prophecy of Daniel, chapter 2, which is concerned with the interpretation of Nebuchadnezzar's dream about a statue. Dante has linked this with Ovid's four ages of man, including the myth of the Golden Age of humankind's innocence and perfect happiness (Crete being considered in antiquity the centre of the Golden Age); and he has introduced his own symbolism of the two legs standing for Empire and Papacy, the right foot of clay representing the corrupt Papacy of his own day.

So far, then, we have a conventional allegorical description; but now comes a truly Dantesque touch, moving in its profundity. Virgil goes on to say that all parts of the body, except the golden head, have cracks in them, from which drip tears. It is these tears that gather and descend to form the stream that Dante sees, and which then drop further into the depths of Hell, giving rise to the three rivers and finally to the frozen lake at the very centre of Hell, in which Dante is later to see the traitors buried up to their necks in the ice. As so often, Dante the poet goes beyond arid allegory to the living depths of human experience. The tears of men and women's sorrows drip through the fissures made by sin down the ages of human history; and the stream of all the misery caused by 'man's inhumanity to man' forms the rivers of the Kingdom of Evil.

It was appropriate that Dante should put this description of the 'old man of Crete' into the mouth of Virgil, the Virgil of *sunt lachrimae rerum et mentum mortalia tangunt* ('there are tears for [human] affairs, and transient humanity touches the heart'). In a single hexameter he expressed much of what I discussed in Chapter I, and also the mysterious connection of evil and sorrow which is the subject of the present chapter. The line (*Aeneid* I 462) is part of Aeneas' reflection as he gazes in tears on the Carthaginian artists' vivid representation of the Trojan War: so much heroism, so much suffering were the consequences of the human evil that had been the cause of the war and of its tragic conclusion for his people. The same can be said of all wars down the ages.

One of the mysterious aspects of evil is that the evil which exists in the human world seems so much greater than the evil that is in the human beings themselves. It is not surprising that so many have believed in a personification of evil – for Christians, traditionally in the form of Lucifer transformed into Satan – a being of immeasurably greater power than the humans whom he influences. It is often hard to believe that even the most wicked of historical figures were evil to a degree commensurate with the evil that they caused. It is not only that a Stalin can be amiably avuncular with children while he sends millions of men and women to their deaths. It is also that there seems to be no proportion between the 'size' of such a human being and the enormity of the evil he can bring about, as Hannah Arendt pointed out in the case of someone like Eichmann. When he was eventually brought to trial in Israel for his part in organizing the Holocaust, the question of punishment seemed somehow irrelevant. The evil was so horrifyingly beyond imagination, the perpetrator so insignificant. There was no way to form an equation of justice.

But there is something else: human beings become caught up in evil. For instance, it may be poverty that drives a man to join the armed forces of a military dictatorship. Soon he is involved in brutal repression or even the torture of his fellow human beings. Again, a good deal in society that is seemingly 'respectable' may in fact be built upon foundations that are morally dubious or clearly evil. This is a frequent theme in the poetry of Ernesto Cardenal, priest and former member of the Sandinista government in Nicaragua. In *Murder Inc.*, for example, a businessman returns in the evening to his luxurious home and enjoys his highball, while he listens to the radio which announces that the police are searching for a criminal. This is no concern of his:

Tú eres una persona decente
un hombre honrado.
*(You are a respectable person, an honest man.)*

But his way of life, his business methods, his lack of concern for justice have contributed to and supported the evils of society; and so the poem ends:

y en tu living-room el radio está hablando de ti.
*(And in your living-room the radio is speaking about you.)*

Even when their own actions are not evil, the conventionally 'good' may condone evil. This often seems to spring more from ignorance or lack of imagination than from malice; but if such blindness is caused by fear of losing vested interests, then surely the responsibility remains. In fact it is difficult for any of us to escape involvement in the structural evils of society. In solidarity with those who suffer we feel a painful impotence to alleviate their suffering and a sense of guilt that we are failing to overcome a selfish inertia. Even more poignant is the dilemma about being accessories in economic injustice. For example, should we buy products made by virtual slave-labour in some Asian countries? It is to our advantage to do so, since they are cheap. Would it help poor young workers if we refused to do so, when the alternative is child-prostitution? But again, does that justify us in being linked to the injustice perpetrated by ruthlessly acquisitive manufacturers? Although it is easy to see how the greed of the economically powerful leads to injustice on a huge scale, the complexities of modern economic structures make it difficult for most of us to have any detailed idea about what could be done to eliminate such injustice. We try to help towards small ameliorations; and for the rest we are left impotently bewailing the situation, and yet feeling guilty. It may be that to bear this is in some small way to have solidarity with those who are actually suffering the injustice. The fact is that we are members of society, and are therefore inevitably involved in the evils of that society. As Harry Williams has remarked, Jesus presumably ate salt, salt which very likely had come from Roman slave-mines.

We are horrified by stories of SS Officers listening to Beethoven in the extermination camps of Nazi Germany. This hideous juxtaposition of beauty and inconceivable inhumanity is an example on the most massive scale ever known of that mysterious interweaving of evil and beauty in human affairs. It was present, for example, in fifteenth-century Florence. I think of the pursuit of beauty in all its forms: the paintings, the sculpture, the buildings, the music, the love of Greek and Latin thought and literature; and then I remember the vicious cruelty with which political opponents were pursued and punished. I think of the young Leonardo da Vinci sitting dispassionately making detailed notes, for a projected painting, of the clothes worn by Bernardo Baroncelli, one of the captured Pazzi conspirators, who was left hanging from a window of the Bargello. Or again, in our own country, there is the extraordinary contrast between the exquisite beauty of Elizabethan and Jacobean poetry and music, and the brutality and squalor of much of everyday life at the same period. I wonder whether some of the audience who crossed London Bridge to see a performance of *Measure for Measure* at the Globe also rode out of the city up Holborn and the Oxford Road to witness the agony of some priest being hanged, drawn and quartered at Tyburn. Always in human affairs there is this intermingling of the sublime and the sordid, of goodness and malice; and so there is in each one of us.

In one of Chesterton's Father Brown stories, the murderer is unmasked by the priest's usual ingenuity. He is aghast and amazed that what he had planned as the perfect crime has been uncovered. When Father Brown recounts to him his motive for the murder and his method of carrying it out, the man cries, 'How can you know these things? Are you a devil?' to which Father Brown replies placidly: 'It is because I have all devils within me'. Not only must we face and acknowledge the evil that we do, but also the even greater evil of which we might be capable under certain circumstances. Because of our solidarity with the whole human race, not only must we suffer with the suffering, hear the cries of the oppressed, acknowledge our involvement with the structural evils of society; but we must also identify with the evil of the oppressor.

Who will deliver us from the evil that we do, the evil in which we become caught up, the evil that we witness?

*

In John 1:29, John the Baptist points to Jesus as the one 'who takes away the sin of the world'. The Latin text changed the Greek singular into the plural *peccata*, 'sins'. In the current English text of the Mass, the singular is restored in the *Gloria*, but the plural occurs again in the 'Lamb of God' and before communion. It could be argued that the change from the singular of the Gospel weakens the force of John the Baptist's proclamation of Christ's redemption of humankind from evil, for the *sin* of the world seems to be of so much greater enormity than the sum of the individual sinful acts; and we are all caught up in it, not only because of our personal sins, but also because we are members of a human society that has evil in its structure. It is true, of course, that Christ can only take away the sins of individual human beings who accept, at least implicitly, their need of redemption; but in St John's Gospel his last words to his disciples before going out from the Last Supper to his passion were 'Take courage; I have conquered the world'. Here 'the world' is to be taken in its Johannine sense of 'the power of evil'. So the good news of the Gospel is that Christ has indeed taken away the sin of the world, even though each human being has to allow this to become true in his or her own life. At this point I am clearly writing out of my faith in the mystery of the redemption. In his second letter to the Corinthians, St Paul wrote, 'For our sake he [God] made the one who knew no sin to be sin, so that we might become the righteousness of God in him' (5:21). This is not just a legal fiction nor the description of a purely symbolic act, like that of Aaron in laying all the sins of the sons of Israel on the scapegoat before it was driven out into the desert (Leviticus 16:20–2). In a real sense Jesus took upon himself the sin of the world. In becoming a human being to redeem humankind he was weighed down by the sins of all people. All Christians, I think, feel deeply about the doctrine of the redemption, for it is the essence of the Good News, although the way it 'works' remains mysterious: how exactly Jesus' life, death and resurrection bring the possibility of salvation to all humankind. St Paul frequently says that Christ died to save us from our sins, and, in Ephesians 5:2, that he gave himself up in our place as a sacrifice to God.

This latter is a main theme in the letter to the Hebrews. Today we still affirm that Christ offered himself as a sacrifice; but perhaps the word has a less vividly physical connotation than it would have had for the early Christians, who were familiar with the religious sacrifices of both Jews and pagans. The scriptural statements about Christ's saving act do not give any explanation of the 'mechanics' of redemption. I suppose most of us of an older generation were brought up on some form of St Anselm's explanation of the efficacy of Christ's sacrifice in terms of 'satisfaction'. Briefly, St Anselm said that Christ's sacrifice of himself in his human nature, being the act of the Son of God, had an infinite value that was sufficient to make satisfaction for the offence of human sin against the infinite majesty of God. This might be called a 'neat' solution, except that it leaves one feeling a little uncomfortable. Although it does not involve any idea of an avenging God who requires propitiation – as scandalized non-Christians and, alas, even some Christians have thought – nevertheless it does seem that such an explanation uses the wrong categories. In fact, St Anselm was thinking in terms of medieval feudalism and considering human 'offence' against God to be like the insult of a serf against the dignity of his lord, for which satisfaction could only be given by one of equal dignity. This seems to put the emphasis in the wrong place. There is no requirement of 'satisfaction' when a parent has been hurt by a child, only an offer of loving sorrow. It seems to me that the mystery of our redemption must somehow lie in the fact that divine love incarnate in a human being was great enough to vanquish human evil ('I have overcome the world'). Divine Love on the cross conquered the evil that put him there; and the proof of his victory was the resurrection. Christ's redemptive love throughout his life led to his death, which was the work of human evil, not something 'required' by the Father.

*

These are a few reflections on a subject that has filled many books. I shall be considering the cross again in Chapter 9; but here I am thinking of how the figure in agony on the cross gives us some idea of what was involved in being 'made sin for our sake'. Even so, it is beyond our capacity to imagine what it was like to be weighed down by the sin of the world. We are both aghast and filled with gratitude at the thought of what Jesus bore for our sake. We think also of our failures to respond to such love.

*Lachrimae amantis*

What is there in my heart that you should sue
so fiercely for its love? What kind of care
brings you as though a stranger to my door
through the long night and in the icy dew

seeking the heart that will not harbour you,
that keeps itself religiously secure?
At this dark solstice filled with frost and fire
your passion's ancient wounds must bleed anew.

So many nights the angel of my house
has fed such urgent comfort through a dream
whispered 'your lord is coming, he is close'

that I have drowsed half-faithful for a time
bathed in pure tones of promise and remorse:
'tomorrow I shall wake to welcome him'

This sonnet by Geoffrey Hill (b. 1932) is the last of a set of seven *Lachrimae*, a title taken from Dowland's twenty-one pieces for viols and lute, published in 1604, of which seven are 'sevean teares figured in sevean passionate pavans'. Dowland's seven pavans are musical expressions of grief, from which Hill takes over the titles for his seven sonnets on aspects of human grief and self-accusation. The sonnet I have quoted is modelled on one by the Spanish dramatist and poet, Lope de Vega (1562–1613). Geoffrey Hill is not a Christian; he has said that he tries to make lyric poetry out of not being able to grasp true religious experience. But he feels deeply the spiritual weight of human evil, and he seems to have a psychological affinity with the religious sensibility of Counter-Reformation Catholicism. Here is a poet with the imaginative ability to express the Christian's grief at failure to respond to his Saviour's love, a love that was ready to suffer on the cross for him and which longs for a loving response. Lacking Lope de Vega's faith, Hill is not able to address the Lord as *Jesús mío*, although he does begin three of the *Lachrimae* sonnets with the apostrophe 'Crucified Lord'. Here he is echoing a famous sixteenth-century sonnet *A Cristo crucificado*, which has sometimes been attributed to St Francis Xavier, without evidence but because its theme is the same as the Latin hymn 'O Deus, ego amo te', which may indeed be his. In both, the poet tells Christ that he loves him not because of any hope of reward or fear of punishment, but simply as a response to the love that Christ has shown for him. (Hopkins translated the Latin hymn into both English and Welsh verse, giving the latter the subtitle *Ochenaid Sant Francis Xavier, Apostol yr Indiaid*, 'The sigh of St Francis Xavier, Apostle of the Indians'.) Although the non-Christian Hill is not able to translate the positive Christian theme, there is in 'Lachrimae amantis' an expression of intense religious emotion. There is also a ruthless unmasking of the evasions of religiosity in the lines '. . . the heart that will not harbour you/that keeps itself *religiously secure*', and in the last tercet where an echo of Keats' 'Nightingale Ode' and 'bathed in pure tones of promise and remorse' imply a critique of the romantically religious and the shallowly devout.

*

Pascal's constant preoccupation with the paradox of the greatness and the wretchedness of humankind, whom he calls 'the glory and the refuse of the universe', leads him to consider the doctrine of original sin (*Pensées* B434). He says that natural reason cannot explain this paradox; humans are a mystery to themselves. On the other hand, the doctrine of the transmission of original sin is shocking to our reason. We are left in a dilemma: without the incomprehensible mystery of that doctrine, we remain incomprehensible to ourselves. Pascal's conclusion is that reason must be silent, so that human beings may learn from revelation what is their true condition: 'by grace made like God and participating in his divinity, and without grace resembling the brute beasts'.

It is difficult for us today to accept the traditional exposition of the theology of original sin because it was stated in terms of monogenesis, the descent of all human beings from one pair, and of a 'fall' from some original perfect state. Our knowledge of an evolutionary world makes this scarcely credible; and yet the term 'original sin' can clearly be seen to refer to a sombre reality, because, as we have been considering, we are all caught up in a 'state of sinfulness', which is indeed original in the sense of arising from the fact of our belonging to the human family.

In chapters 2 and 3 of Genesis, the writer is expressing in the best way that was available to him a fundamental truth about the human condition: human beings are not 'as they ought to be', and in particular, they are not in the right relation to their Creator. The author described what they *ought* to be like in terms of a perfect state in the Garden of Eden before the 'fall'. We find the concept of a prelapsarian earthly paradise more than improbable; and St Paul in chapter 5 of his letter to the Romans gives us some help. Instead of comparing a fallen

Adam with a previously perfect Adam, he contrasts a sinful Adam (though he does still speak of a 'fall') with the sinless Christ. In other words, instead of looking *back* to a supposed state of perfection in Eden, he looks *forward* to what human beings can become through grace: images of Christ.

Both the author of Genesis 2 and 3 and St Paul assume the descent of all humans from one pair. For us today monogenesis seems unlikely; but I think that behind the idea there lies an important truth, namely the unity of the human race. Nowadays we see more clearly that a human being is only fully defined as a subject of relationships. The concept of the unity of the human race is more truly expressed by the recognition of the mutual relationships between its members than by any supposed common descent from a unique pair. We can say that every child that is born is the subject of what we call original sin simply by virtue of belonging to the human race. 'Original sin' expresses the recognition of humankind's fundamental need of redemption; and this has to be seen in terms of a framework of personal relationships. It is indeed, as Pascal recognized, very mysterious. We are created and destined for love, and yet we are 'spoiled' by a profound egotism. As Tillich has pointed out, we suffer from a triple estrangement: from ourselves, from others and from God. Somehow this is the inheritance of every child born into the human family. Sin has taken root in the human community and it is from this 'sin of the world' that every individual needs redemption. It was to achieve this that the Word was made flesh. He bore the burden of the sin of the world and through his infinite love he has liberated us from it.

In our life of faith there is always tension. Our gratitude for what Christ has done for us does not exclude sorrow for our contribution to the sum of human evil and for our failure to respond to his love:

Drop, drop, slow tears
   And bathe those beauteous feet
Which brought from Heaven
   The news and Prince of Peace:
Cease not, wet eyes,
   His mercy to entreat;
To cry for vengeance
   Sin doth never cease.
In your deep floods
   Drown all my faults and fears;
Nor let His eye
   See sin, but through my tears.

Phineas Fletcher (1582–1650)

# 7

# The Silence of God

O that thou shouldst give dust a tongue
To crie to thee,
And then not heare it crying! . . .
George Herbert: 'Deniall'

THE PERSECUTION OF Christians in seventeenth-century Japan provides the setting for the novel *Silence* by the Catholic Japanese writer, Shusaku Endo. From the time of St Francis Xavier's landing on the Japanese coast in 1549 until almost the end of the century, the Jesuit missionaries were favourably received by local rulers, and their efforts bore fruit to the extent that within forty years Japanese Christians numbered about 300,000. But then came the first outburst of persecution, largely motivated by xenophobia and leading to the crucifixion in 1597 of twenty-six Christians, St Paul Miki and his companions. In 1614 an edict was issued for the expulsion of all foreign missionaries. Priests continued to enter the country and to work underground; but the authorities were determined to wipe out Christianity, and both Japanese Christians and European missionairies suffered appallingly cruel tortures and death. Until 1632 no missionary had apostatized; but then, Christovao Ferreira, the Portuguese Provincial of the Jesuits, gave way. It was a grievous shock to the Christian community to learn that the leader of the mission had apostatized and that he was said to be collaborating with his former persecutors. Although Japan was by now officially cut off from the outside world, more missionaries did manage to enter the country. In 1643 a group of ten came; but they were soon captured, and all apostatized after terrible tortures, although most of them later revoked their apostasy.

It is on one of these priests that Endo has based his Portuguese Jesuit, Fr Rodrigues. Soon after landing in Japan, he and a companion are warned by local Christians that officials are searching both for native Christians and for foreign missionaries; so the two Jesuits remain in hiding in a hut within sight of the sea. Two Christians from the nearby village are apprehended, and, on refusing to apostatize, are tied to trees which are set on the seashore in such a way that at high tide the water reaches up to the prisoners' necks. The two priests in their hiding place watch as these martyrs die a lingering death over the space of two days. Father Rodrigues reports all this in a letter which he hopes to be able to send back to his superiors. He reflects on the grief he felt at the sufferings of these Japanese peasant Christians:

> What do I want to say? I myself do not quite understand. Only that today, when for the glory of God Mokichi and Ichizo moaned, suffered and died, I cannot bear the monotonous sound of the dark sea gnawing at the shore. Behind the depressing silence of this sea, the silence of God . . . the feeling that while men raise their voices in anguish, God remains with folded arms, silent.

Here Endo introduces one of the main themes of the novel: the silence of God when his human creature most needs the reassurance of his presence and care.

It is not long before Rodrigues is betrayed by a renegade Christian and imprisoned in a hut. In his loneliness and fear in face of what is in store for him, he repeatedly ponders the mystery of God's impenetrable silence. He wonders whether

Jesus in the Garden of Gethsemane had also felt the silence of God. The magistrate plays a cat-and-mouse game with him, sometimes friendly, sometimes threatening. When the priest has been 'softened up' and demoralized in this way, the magistrate confronts him with Ferreira, the historical Jesuit Provincial who had apostatized years before. Endo makes his fictional Father Rodrigues to be a former student of Ferreira in the seminary in Portugal and to have had a great reverence for him as teacher and priest. A defeated Ferreira tells Rodrigues how he came to apostatize. For days Rodrigues has heard moaning sounds outside his hut-prison. Now Ferreira explains that these sounds are the groans of Christians suspended upside down over a pit filled with excrement. He says that years before he himself had been in exactly Rodrigues' situation in that same prison and hearing similar moans. He declares that he had not agreed to put his foot on the image of Christ (the sign of apostasy insisted on by the authorities) because of his own sufferings in the pit torture, but because he was promised that, if he apostatized, those he heard moaning would immediately be released from their sufferings. Listening to Ferreira, Rodrigues is in an agony at the appalling dilemma that will face him also.

> A great shadow passed over his soul, like that of the wings of a bird flying over the mast of a ship. The wings of the bird now brought to his mind the memory of the various ways in which the Christians had died. At that time, too, God had been silent. When the misty rain floated over the sea, he was silent. When the one-eyed man had been killed beneath the blazing rays of the sun, he had said nothing. At that time . . . he had been able to thrust the terrible doubt far from the threshold of his mind. But now it was different. Why is God continually silent while these groaning voices go on?

When the time comes, Rodrigues, like Ferreira, in order to

save the other prisoners from further torture, carries out the act of apostasy by putting his foot on the metal image of Christ; and, like Ferreira, he then has to spend the remainder of his empty years in shame as a tool of the authorities, living in the style of a Japanese and always at their beck and call.

Endo presents in the anguish of his protagonist a limiting case of the bewilderment that we all feel: if there is a God, why does he remain silent and allow all the evil in the world and all the suffering that his creatures experience? Of course, it is a limiting case that is not confined to fiction. We are apt to forget what darkness must at times envelop those who are suffering, and perhaps awaiting death, for the sake of their fundamental moral convictions. How sorely Thomas More must have been tried by the well-intentioned urgings of family and friends that he should accede to King Henry VIII's demands. In our own day, those who face imprisonment and torture for the sake of conscience must sometimes say to themselves: 'Why wasn't I content just to lead my own quiet life, without getting involved in trying to defend the poor or to work for freedom in society?' That can for many translate into: 'Why does God remain silent and allow me to suffer because I am trying to do his will?'

This is the particular dilemma of those who are suffering for the sake of justice; but we all face the problem of trying to make sense of the evil and the pain in the world. Since the eighteenth century this has provided a principal argument for denying the existence of God. As Hume argued: 'If there were a benevolent God, he would wish his creatures to be perfectly happy; and if he were omnipotent he would be able to make them so. But men are not perfectly happy. Therefore . . .' Of course, there are still many, as in earlier centuries, who believe there is a God, while they anguish at the pain of the world or in their own sufferings. Is it possible to reconcile this experience with Dante's talk about love as the centre of reality?

*

The classical biblical exposition of the problem is the book of Job, which was probably written in the fifth century BC, long before the Jews had any belief in a happy future life (a belief that only became current in the second century). Nor obviously could the author draw on any concept of the redemptive value of human suffering united to the sufferings of Christ. At that period there was the simplistic view: a prosperous and happy life equated with virtuous behaviour, misfortune and suffering with evil-doing. The book of Job is essentially didactic, although it may be based on the life of a real person who had lived at an earlier period.

In the prose prologue God allows Satan to test the virtuous Job with a series of calamities to see whether he will remain faithful to God. Job loses in succession possessions, family and health. At first he accepts all this patiently as coming from the hand of God. Then, as he sits in the ash pit scraping his ulcered body with a potsherd, three friends come to him and in turn put forward the traditional doctrine that, if an individual suffers, it is because he has offended God. But Job protests his innocence and curses the day he was born. The friends turn against him and berate him for what they claim must be a guilty conscience and a failure to admit his sins. Job continues to insist that he is innocent, and he cannot understand why God is treating him so harshly; but he admits that human beings are not in a position to question the Creator's actions, since God is judge as well as defendant in his own case. Through the long dialogue with his friends, Job's mood varies from humble acceptance that God's actions are beyond human comprehension to rebelliousness at his apparently unjust treatment. It is God, not his own sinfulness, that is the cause of his sufferings. Moreover, Job is tormented by God's absence:

If I go eastward, he is not there;
or westward – still I cannot see him.
If I seek him in the north, he is not to be found,
invisible still when I turn to the south. (23:8–9)

– and yet he *is* there:

. . . he knows of every step I take! (23:10)

God is present, but he is silent:

I cry to you, and you give me no answer . . . (30:20)

Finally God *does* give Job an answer (chs. 38–9). To evoke the awesome power of the divine creator, the author describes Yahweh as speaking to Job 'from the heart of the tempest'. He overwhelms Job with a torrent of words in hectoring tones:

Brace yourself like a fighter;
now it is my turn to ask questions and yours to inform me.
Where were you when I laid the earth's foundations?
Tell me, since you are so well informed!
. . . Have you an inkling of the extent of the earth?
Tell me all about it if you have! (38:3–4, 18)

The whole speech, in which Yahweh repeatedly asks Job what he can know about the secrets of creation, is a wonderful evocation of the beauty and magnificence of the created world:

Who laid [the earth's] cornerstone
when all the stars of the morning were singing with joy,
and the Sons of God in chorus were chanting praise?
. . . Can you fasten the harness of the Pleiades,
or untie Orion's bands?
. . . Can your voice carry as far as the clouds
and make the pent-up waters do your bidding?

. . . Does the eagle soar at your command
to make her eyrie in the heights? (38:6–7, 31, 34; 39:27)

Having battered him with a series of withering rhetorical questions,

> Yahweh turned to Job and he said:
> Is the Lord's opponent ready to give in?
> Has God's critic thought up an answer?
> Job replied to Yahweh:
> My words have been frivolous: what can I reply?
> I had better put my finger on my lips. (40:1–4)

The book ends with Yahweh expressing his displeasure towards Job's three friends and restoring Job's fortunes, granting him more possessions than he had before calamity struck him and a new family of sons and daughters.

The author of the book of Job was struggling with the inadequacy of the traditional Judaic solution to the problem of suffering at about the same period that in Greece the great writers of tragedy were expressing the same problem in the context of ineluctable Fate. Since God finally rewards Job with even greater material prosperity and happiness than he enjoyed before Satan was given permission to put him to the test, it looks at first sight as though the author has ultimately had to fall back on the traditional doctrine. This, however, is not so. He had no other way available to symbolize God's approval of Job; but the important point is that God 'burns with anger' against the friends who have consistently put forward the traditional view, 'for not speaking truthfully about me as my servant Job has done' (42:7–8). The book of Job makes a very significant advance from the simplistic equation of prosperity with obedience to God's law. By the end of the book Job has recognized that God's ways are beyond the understanding of men and women. He has experienced the mystery of God; and, convinced of the littleness of humankind in the presence of his creator, he is ready to accept in adoration that God cannot be 'tied down' by the limited views of human beings. This conclusion has been foreshadowed in an earlier chapter (28), which is a poem in praise of wisdom. Human beings use their ingenuity to make use of the riches of the earth and to search out the secrets of nature; but 'where does wisdom come from? . . . It is outside the knowledge of every living thing . . . God alone has traced its path' (vv. 20–1, 23). (This chapter might be salutary reading for some overconfident scientists.)

Another point which we may take to heart is that Job is not blamed for his moments of rebelliousness. Indeed he encounters God *at the end* of his revolt. So the book expresses a double paradox: fidelity to the law is no sure protection against the mysterious gratuitousness of God's action, and the impatient Job is restored to prosperity, while God's 'defenders' are rejected.

*

In this chapter I am struggling with two questions, distinct but inseparable: Why does God allow suffering? Why does God always remain silent? In Endo's *Silence* the emphasis is on the second, in the book of Job on the first, although inevitably in each case both questions arise.

A modern poet, a priest of the Church in Wales, who is much preoccupied with these questions is R.S. Thomas (b. 1913), especially in three volumes which he published in the 1970s. For this poet the silence of God is most usually seen as an absence or else as a presence that continually eludes the human searcher:

> Why no! I never thought other than
> That God is that great absence
> In our lives, the empty silence

Within, the place where we go
Seeking, not in hope to
Arrive or find. He keeps the interstices
In our knowledge, the darkness
Between stars.

(from 'Via Negativa')

We have here, not the discredited 'God of the gaps' but 'God in the gaps'. A scientific age has been inclined to dismiss belief in the existence of God as being merely a way to explain what in human experience and observation seemed otherwise inexplicable, and to claim that science is successfully pushing back the boundaries of all the 'gaps' that require explanation. In this context we may note that R.S. Thomas has also been preoccupied by the problem of finding a valid religious language in an age of science and technology; and he sees this problem paralleled by the difficulty of finding God in an age when men and women are only interested in verifiable facts:

. . . astronaut
on impossible journeys
to the far side of the self
I return with messages
I cannot decipher, garrulous
about them, worrying the ear
of the passer-by, hot on his way
to the marriage of plain fact with plain fact.

(from 'The New Mariner')

Paradoxically, the presence of God can only be experienced in his absence:

It is this great absence
that is like a presence, that compels

me to address it without hope
of a reply. It is a room I enter

from which someone has just
gone, the vestibule for the arrival
of one who has not yet come. . . .

What resource have I
other than the emptiness without him of my whole
being, a vacuum he may not abhor?

(from 'The Absence')

The last lines may seem to provide evidence for those who think that humans 'invent' a God to try to fill the emptiness that they feel at the centre of their being; but I do not believe that this is so. I think that here, as so often, Thomas is expressing in his characteristically tentative way, an aspect of apophatic theology, so-called 'negative theology' (note the title of his 'Via Negativa'), the paradoxical knowledge of the Unknowable, as in so much of the writings of the mystics; for instance the anonymous fourteenth-century *Cloud of Unknowing*. There will be more to be said about this in the chapter on prayer.

R.S. Thomas does sometimes express the positive experience of God's presence: as for instance in 'The Bright Field', where he uses the image of the sun breaking through the clouds and lighting up a field. He says that such moments of awareness of God's presence seem transitory but are really outside time. On the whole, however, Thomas is a Christian poet of the *via negativa*. Like Simone Weil, he sees the task of men and women to be a 'waiting on God'. Corresponding to God's absence and presence is the human vocation to watch and to pray; and as the presence is *in* the absence, so the praying is in the waiting and watching.

*

It is difficult to know what light can be thrown on the great mystery of human suffering and God's silence. One thing is sure: it will not do to put forward the pious, anodyne solution that all will be well in some future life. Incidentally, the whole idea of religion as consolation in that sense will not do. On the contrary, Christian faith is a formidable challenge to which most of us do not fully respond. For myself, I think that, if I did not believe in the Christian revelation, it is possible that I might not believe in any form of human survival beyond the grave and yet still be convinced that there was a God. For many the suffering in the world is reason enough to deny the existence of God; but for others of us even that appalling sum of suffering and the eternal silence of God are not sufficient to shake our conviction of the existence of God as the ground of all being. Like Job, we are left to wrestle with trying to reconcile the two.

I wonder whether perhaps we ask the wrong questions. Careful though traditional theism may be to preserve God's 'simplicity' by insisting that his attributes are not separable, we do in practice tend to think of omnipotence and divine love as separate, and so to present ourselves with the dilemma of considering an all-powerful loving God who 'allows' so much evil and suffering in his created world. At the beginning of his *Summa Theologica* St Thomas Aquinas emphasizes that, strictly speaking, since we have no direct rational knowledge of God, we can only discuss what God is *not*, not what he is. We can only attempt to speak negatively of his being by removing from our concepts the limitations that exist in all created perfections. Nevertheless, theology does become quasi-deductive and positive when it goes on to discuss God's goodness, omnipotence, immutability, and so on. I now find that, despite its admirable logical coherence, traditional theology does not always seem to correspond to the reality that we experience. Different ways of thought and of experience are appropriate to different periods. I think that many in the late twentieth century have to try to find God in his absence; and that the more fruitful reflection on God and the world is intuitive, rather than through the rationalism of our hellenistic inheritance. We have to begin from our experience of what existence is like, without trying to make everything fit in with apparently valid conclusions about God's omnipotence or immutability.

We are accustomed to the idea often expressed in a very human fashion: God, in wishing to create beings with free will had to 'take the risk' that his human creatures would abuse that freedom, thus bringing moral evil into the world. It will have been pointed out also to many of us in Religious Studies courses that even God cannot do what is logically impossible: he cannot, for instance, make a square circle. Perhaps these two ideas can be brought together. Modern physics relies on mathematics for its description of nature, and ultimately mathematics is the mathematics of logic. Is the universe then the way it is out of logical necessity? Theists usually consider that God, for reasons hidden from us, has made this particular universe out of an infinite range of possible universes; but I wonder whether one might not argue somewhat differently. If God wanted to have a universe in which there were free intelligent creatures capable of love, is this the only universe that he could have created? If God cannot do what is logically impossible and if this universe with its particular physical laws is the only logically possible one which could allow for the evolution of human beings, then perhaps, just as he was prepared to risk men and women loving wrongly, so God was also prepared to make this world with all the suffering it contains, in order that there might be creatures who could love and ultimately be united to him. This is an intriguing line of thought, although in view of what I have said in the Introduction, I suppose the question would arise as to which system of logic is the logic of reality, if indeed there is one single system that fits all reality.

*

There is a good example in Graham Greene's *The Honorary Consul* of what I have said about the evil and the suffering of the world leading one man to cease believing in God, while they cause another to agonize because he is unable not to believe in God. Eduardo Plarr and Leon Rivas had been boyhood friends at a Jesuit school in Paraguay. Years later in northern Argentina, Dr Plarr finds himself the prisoner of a reluctant captor, the priest-turned-revolutionary, Fr Rivas. While they are hiding in a hut, waiting for the police to close in, they discuss these matters. Plarr had long ago given up any belief in God, partly because of the human suffering he had witnessed as a doctor. The suffering of the poor through gross social injustice had led Leon Rivas to become a revolutionary, but had not destroyed his belief in God and Christ. His experience, however, had forced him to reject the purely benign deity of conventional Christianity. He admits that his thoughts may be wild, but 'I can see no other way to believe in God. The God I believe in must be responsible for all the evil as well as for all the saints. He has to be a God made in our image with a night-side as well as a day-side.' He believes in Christ and the redemption, but also that God creates monsters like Hitler and destroys children and cities.

The idea of a night-side of God may be a 'wild thought', but we have to face the question whether God is in some sense responsible for evil and suffering. In the scholastic tradition, evil is defined negatively as *privatio boni*, a lack of due good; but this does not seem to correspond adequately with the facts. Nor do I think that it is sufficient to say that God merely 'permits' evil. There are positive evils, and I think that we must say that God causes them. There seems to be scriptural warrant for this view: 'I form the light and create the dark. I make good fortune and create calamity, it is I, Yahweh, who do all this' (Isaiah 45:7, where, I understand, the same Hebrew word is used for 'create' as in the creation narratives of Genesis). In fact, there are many passages, not only in the Old Testament but right up to the book of Revelation, in which God is said to *cause* suffering to human beings; and I do not think it would be correct to read these as imprecise statements about God permitting suffering to befall men and women. It seems to me to be more truly religious to begin from our human experience, as the biblical writers did, than to attempt deductions about the nature of God from metaphysical postulates.

If I understand correctly, it can be said that, although in popular Hinduism most worshippers are devotees of either Vishnu or Shiva, each with varied attributes, these two can also be considered, not as separate gods, but as two manifestations of the Supreme. When that is the case, Vishnu is seen as the Preserver and Shiva as the Destroyer, together with Brahma the Creator. These are then three aspects of the one supreme God, in which Brahma and Vishnu correspond with our ideas of divine transcendence and immanence and Shiva with Leon Rivas' 'night-side of God'. I take it that the Indian mind is content to have the concepts of Vishnu the Preserver and Shiva the Destroyer remaining side by side without any attempt at synthesis. Our western rationalistic outlook insists on seeking logical coherence; and it is here that I struggle with the possibility of essential paradox at the heart of reality, even divine reality.

However great the perplexity and anguish that we experience because of human suffering and the silence of God, there *are* positive things that can be said. First of all, it does seem that some degree of suffering is necessary to bring a human being to maturity. We do not know why this should be; and we may feel that, if we were in charge of the universe, we would arrange things otherwise. But that is the way it is; and out of pain can come great beauty. There is the heroic grandeur of those who have come through much suffering; and at a more modest level, there is beauty in a human face that reflects the experience of life, the difficulties and the pains as well as the joys. Of course, this does not 'justify God's ways to men', when we think of Auschwitz or the appalling pain that some have to bear in illness. It is mysterious how intense suffering can break one person and 'make' another. If in the latter case at least we can see a meaning in the suffering, can we be sure that there is not a meaning in the other case?

A further point is that God does not always seem to be absent in times of suffering. On the contrary, one can be powerfully conscious of God's presence in the most painful situation, when all seems to be falling apart. There can be a most strong conviction that he is present *in* the situation, not as a consolation to take away the pain, but as a challenge to live through it:

> Thou hast bound bones and veins in me, fastened me
> flesh,
> And after it almost unmade, what with dread,
> Thy doing: and dost thou touch me afresh?
> Over again I feel thy finger and find thee.
> (G. M. Hopkins: 'The Wreck of the Deutschland')

Of course, that conviction is not always there; in the darkness of desolation God may indeed seem to be absent. As C.S. Lewis wrote in *A Grief Observed* after the death of his wife: 'Go to him when your need is desperate, and what do you find? A door slammed in your face . . . Silence . . . The longer you wait, the more emphatic the silence will become.' In view of these opposite experiences of God's apparent presence or absence, the sceptic may well conclude that the conviction of God's presence in times of distress is just something that a person invents as a consolation. I can only say that the consciousness of God's presence at such periods, not as a consolation but as a challenge, can be so deep that it is impossible to believe that it is fabricated.

From an explicitly Christian point of view we can add something more. It is not just that Jesus has given us an example of how to bear suffering in patience and with an active submission to God's mysterious will. We believe that he is united to us in our sufferings, as we are to him in his passion. By baptism we are in a true way united to Christ in his death and resurrection.

> We are in difficulties on all sides, but never cornered; we see no answer to our problems, but never despair . . . always we carry with us in our body the death of Jesus, so that the life of Jesus, too, may always be seen in our body. Indeed, while we are still alive, we are consigned to our death every day, for the sake of Jesus, so that in our mortal flesh the life of Jesus, too, may be openly shown. (2 Corinthians 4:8–11)

This is a theme which St Paul comes back to frequently: 'All I want is to know Christ and the power of his resurrection, and to share his sufferings by reproducing the pattern of his death' (Philippians 3:10). Not only are our sufferings united to those of Christ, but they are co-redemptive with his: 'I rejoice in my sufferings on your behalf, and in my body I complete what is still to be undergone by Christ for the sake of his body, the Church' (Colossians 1:24).

In times of great darkness, St Paul's positive attitude may seem meaningless, as Fr Rodrigues discovered. Nevertheless, God is not always silent, though the culmination of his self-revelation is mysterious indeed: a cry from the cross.

# 8

# 'My God, My God, Why Have You Forsaken Me?'

WHAT ARE WE TO MAKE of that cry of dereliction from the cross? In what sense was God the Son abandoned by the Father in his ultimate agony? We have now reached the central mystery, which we can only approach tentatively and reverently.

The Gospels which have come down to us are the written record of the reflections of the first Christian communities on the facts of the life, death and resurrection of Jesus. The narratives of his passion and death reveal differences of perception, or at least of emphasis. Mark's account, closely followed by Matthew, is one of stark realism in its description of Jesus' suffering from the hour of his agony in the garden of Gethsemane to the moment of his death on the cross. Luke puts less emphasis on the distress of Jesus, although he does make his own contribution: 'In his anguish he prayed even more earnestly, and his sweat fell to the ground like great drops of blood' (22:43–4). By the time John was writing, theological reflection on the divinity of Christ led to a depiction of a Jesus almost serene in his control of the situation, even as he went to his death.

Jesus' agony begins among the olive trees of Gethsemane, when he foresees the horrors that are to come and prays for deliverance from them, yet accepting his Father's will. The evangelists do not dwell on the details of the cruelties of crucifixion, which were well known to those living in the Roman

Empire of the first century. Crucifixion itself was preceded by savage and unlimited lashing with a whip furnished with pieces of lead or bone to tear the flesh, and administered by brutal soldiers, who then drove the naked victims through the streets carrying their own crosses. Jesus was spared none of the horror of it. 'In the days of his flesh, he offered prayers and entreaties with loud cries and tears to him who had the power to save him from death' (Hebrews 5:7).

In the garden his extreme distress was surely caused not only by the natural fear of the suffering and agonizing death that were about to befall him. What anguish there must have been in the knowledge that his love had been rejected and in the crushing weight of the thought that his whole mission had seemingly failed. The climax of that anguish came at the moment of the cry of dereliction from the cross: 'My God, my God, why have you forsaken me?' It is with what lay behind these words that I am here concerned. I am taking it – as seems to be generally accepted – that this quotation of the opening words of Psalm 22 (21) as reported in Mark and Matthew is an authentic saying of Jesus, unlike some or all of the other 'seven last words', which many exegetes take to be the expression of early Christian reflection on the character of Jesus and his redemptive work. The last third of the psalm changes from being the lament of a man who feels abandoned by God into a thanksgiving for God's loving care. (The evangelists use some of the earlier verses in their description of episodes on Golgotha: the jeering of the passers-by, the casting of lots for Jesus' clothing.) In view of the whole context from Gethsemane onwards, it seems to me unlikely that, as has sometimes been suggested, Jesus was intending to quote the whole psalm with its positive conclusion. We are left with the mystery of those words forced from his dying lips. What does it mean when a divine person cries out that he is forsaken by God?

As creatures gifted with intelligence, it is right that we should struggle to understand what we can of this mystery. I shall first summarize what traditional Thomist theology has to say. St Thomas Aquinas unfolds the implications of the definitions of the Council of Chalcedon (AD 451), which state that Jesus Christ was truly God and truly man, and that in him the two natures were united in one divine person, the properties of each nature remaining distinct. I am concerned here with what Aquinas has to say about the immutability and impassibility of God in the context of the incarnation and of the sufferings of Christ. He concludes that we can truly assert that God became a human being because a divine person assumed a complete human nature, and that this does not imply any change in the Godhead but only in the human nature that was assumed. In his discussion of Christ's sufferings, St Thomas says that the whole soul of Christ suffered in its essence and in its powers, and yet did not lose the joy of the beatific vision of God. In answer to the objection that, if Christ's whole soul was suffering, it could not at the same time enjoy the beatific vision, he says that it is possible for the superior reason to enjoy blessedness while the lower reason experiences the pain of suffering. When he asks whether Christ's suffering is to be predicated of his divinity, Aquinas answers in the negative. He reminds us of the definition of Chalcedon, that the two natures and their properties remain distinct in the one divine person; and he concludes that the divine person of Christ did indeed suffer, but only in his human nature, not in his divine nature, which is impassible. St Thomas' only two references to Jesus' cry of dereliction on the cross are somewhat peripheral. In both places he simply says that it was the result of his Father's will not to protect him from his persecutors.

St Thomas' theological position in this part of the *Summa* is, as always, admirably coherent and consistent. The Second Person of the Trinity, absolutely immutable and impassible in his Godhead, is really mutable and passible in his humanity. He who suffers is God, but it is in his humanity only that he suffers. However, this traditional line of thought, logically consistent though it is, does not correspond to what seems to me must in some way be the reality. I am not just referring to what may be an obsolete Chalcedonian terminology or outmoded medieval psychology. I have a conviction that God's being is more closely involved in suffering, difficult though this makes it to preserve usually accepted logic.

The Thomist position means that God suffered in a human nature for a short period nearly two thousand years ago. I am convinced that, because of his unlimited love for us, God is somehow 'more permanently' involved in the sufferings of the world. Perhaps one could say that the Second Person of the Trinity continues to suffer in the human nature of Jesus Christ. Maybe that is what Pascal had in mind when he wrote, 'Jesus will be in agony until the end of the world; we must not sleep during that time', and when in the same *pensée* he has Jesus say, 'Do you want me always to pay with the blood of my humanity without your shedding any tears?' (B553). But I would want to go even further. Somehow, as R.S. Thomas expresses it in various ways in a number of his poems, there is an eternal wound in the side of God. Origen (d. c. 250) may not always be the most orthodox of theologians, but this remarkable passage provides us with food for reflection:

> The Redeemer took our sufferings upon himself before he endured the Cross – indeed even before he deigned to take our flesh. If he had not felt these sufferings, he would not have come to partake of our human life. What was this passion he suffered for us beforehand? It was the passion of love. But the Father himself, the God of the universe, who is full of long-suffering and plenteous in mercy and sympathy, does he not also suffer in a certain

> way? . . . He suffers the sufferings of love. (Homilies in Ezekiel 6:6)

Whenever we are struggling to think about God we are considering the ultimate mystery of reality, just as much in the question of his immutability and impassibility as in the revealed mysteries of the incarnation and Trinity. I do not find it too difficult to accept that God's knowledge of his changing creation is itself unchanging. I can conceive of his knowledge, as it were, encompassing the whole history of the evolving universe in one eternal glance. But I cannot believe that his love is content in the timeless knowledge that in the end all will be well for his creatures, or that he does not suffer in his love for his creation. The usual position taken up by Western theology is to say, 'In the end we are faced with mystery and can say no more; but what we have been able to say is at least logically consistent and non-contradictory.' What I want to say is: 'In the end there is mystery, and in trying to approach it, we meet irreducible paradox which will sometimes involve a statement and its negation.' I shall return to this question of logic later in the chapter; but first let us look further at what revelation tells us, without being restricted to the deductions made from it by traditional theology.

'His state was divine, yet he did not cling to his equality with God, but emptied himself to assume the condition of a slave, and became as men are' (Philippians 2:6–7). Here we have the mystery of kenosis, the emptying of the Son in becoming a human being. Clearly, in one sense his divinity was hidden in a finite human nature; but this does not mean that the kenosis was an emptying out of his divinity. The incarnation was not a de-divinization, since he who assumed a human nature was still a divine person. Jesus shows us in a finite way what the infinite God is truly like; he is not just a human 'model' of what God is like. When Philip asks him to show his disciples the Father, Jesus answers, 'He who has seen me *has* seen the Father . . . Do you not believe that I am in the Father and the Father is in me?' (John 14:8–10) So St Paul writes to the Colossians that Christ 'is the image of the unseen God' (1:15), and again that 'in him dwells all the fulness of the Godhead bodily' (2:9); and in the introduction to the letter to the Hebrews we read: 'In the last days God has spoken to us through his Son . . . the perfect copy of his nature' (1:2–3). The incarnation is not a temporary disguise of God; it reveals his very essence. Jesus shows us in time what God is like eternally.

We are unfortunately so accustomed to thinking of power in terms of domination that this is how we expect God to manifest his infinite power. Instead, on the cross he shows his omnipotence in love, not in domination. We are aware of the vulnerability that accompanies all human love. The cross shows us that this is true of divine love also. The God who loves allows himself to suffer in solidarity with the suffering of his creatures, and he puts himself at the mercy of human folly and wickedness, not only on Calvary but throughout the whole history of the world.

The mystery of the suffering of God is at its most acute in Jesus' cry of dereliction from the cross. As I have said, this almost certainly represents an authentic saying of Jesus, even to being preserved in Aramaic. Far from being the result of theological reflection in the early Christian community, it has left an intractable theological problem ever since. A human nature was suffering appalling physical and mental agony; but it was a person who cried out, and that person was divine. What can it mean when God is abandoned by God?

The only way that we can make any sense of it is to see it in trinitarian terms. The Christian believes that there is a mysterious distinction within the Godhead. Within the Trinity, God is eternally self-communicating love, and in the kenosis of the incarnation he is self-emptying love for the sake of the human race: 'God loved the world so much that he gave his only Son' (John 3:16). The Father lets the Son sacrifice himself through the Spirit who is love. Only the Son died on the cross, but surely Father and Spirit must have suffered in his suffering. In speaking of these things we can hardly know what our words might mean; but the cross belongs essentially to the Christian belief in the trinitarian God. During Jesus' last hours, some sort of darkness seems to have hidden the Father from him, beginning in Gethsemane and ending with that terrible cry from the cross. There, I think, we have reached a depth of mystery and paradox about which we can say no more. All we can do is to try to hold in tension the revelation that on the cross God was both present ('God in Christ was reconciling the world to himself', 2 Corinthians 5:19) and absent.

*

It has often been remarked that heresies have tended to arise when some paradox of faith has been avoided by denying one aspect of revealed truth. So, for example, in the early centuries, Docetists, Arians, Nestorians variously denied either the full humanity or the full divinity of Jesus Christ. The Christology of some contemporary theologians seems to present Jesus simply as a man who came to be filled with the Spirit of God. On the other hand, I think that, generally speaking, Roman Catholic devotion has tended to stress the divinity of Christ to such an extent that his full humanity is ignored, except in the context of the sufferings of Jesus in his passion. It seems fair to say that most Catholics keep these two aspects of their devotional life distinct, not adverting to the logical and theological problems involved in the conjunction of the two.

In his fine book, *Love's Endeavour, Love's Expense* (1977), W.H. Vanstone proposes the model of God as the perfect artist. An artist 'sets himself problems' by the very choice of artistic form for the work he is creating. So Vanstone suggests that the divine act of creation is precarious and in that sense the Creator is vulnerable, although he has the power and the will to regain control and resolve the problems. Similarly, since love is essentially self-giving and therefore vulnerable, Vanstone maintains that the kenosis of God must mean that 'for the being of the universe, God is totally expended, expended in endless and precarious endeavour'. This idea of God as perfect artist and perfect lover is most attractive; but it seems to me to lead, if less obviously, to a difficulty similar to that of A.N. Whitehead's process theology. It seems to imply an evolutionary God, even though Vanstone does speak briefly of the endless being of God within the Trinity. He says explicitly that God's activity in creation is a step into the unknown, although he adds that lost control is regained by renewed creative activity. It may be that it is only a lifetime's assumption that divine reality is eternal and non-successive that makes it difficult for me to accept that God does not know what is going to happen. As I have already said, I do not find it impossible to conceive of God's eternal knowledge encompassing in one non-successive act the whole evolving history of the universe. This would not affect the free will of human beings, whose acts are carried out in time. Nor do I think that the radical unpredictabilities of the physical world revealed by modern quantum mechanics or chaos theory give any reason to change this view.

John Polkinghorne, formerly Professor of Mathematical Physics at Cambridge and now an Anglican minister, is – rightly, I believe – more concerned than Vanstone to keep explicitly in view the inevitable dialectical tension between the God of unfolding history and the transcendent God of a timeless act. (See *Science and Providence*, 1989.) He speaks of a dipolar God, who is both the God of being and the God of becoming; and he points out that this concept of polarity is really a holding in tension of the traditional ideas of God's transcendence and his immanence. Nevertheless, Polkinghorne is close to Vanstone when he writes: 'It does not seem conceivable that the omniscient God can know with certainty the unformed future.' He holds that even God cannot know the future because human beings are truly free to choose and because of the inbuilt unpredictability within both the microcosm of quantum mechanics and the complex dynamical systems of chaos theory; so that neither human action nor the unfolding physical universe can be known beforehand. I have said that I do not see that it is necessary to put any restriction on God's knowledge for these reasons. To do so would seem to confuse two modes of reality, the eternal and the temporal.

As both scientist and theologian, Polkinghorne is concerned to preserve consistency of thought, and he speaks of *apparent* contradictions that have to be held in tension by the Christian faith. I wonder, however, whether what we have to face are not apparent contradictions but irreducible paradoxes. I may seem to have strayed a long way from meditation on Christ's cry of dereliction; but it is here above all that I wonder about traditional logic and the law of non-contradiction. I have only read one or two of the recent works which claim to produce systems of formal logic in which, under certain conditions, it is possible to assert something is true and to assert that it is false. For instance, N. Rescher and R. Brandon in *The Logic of Inconsistency* (1979) construct a logical world in which it is possible to assert the truth of proposition p and to assert the truth of not-p. The authors claim that it is possible for such 'singularities' to exist locally, as it were, without causing global logical collapse. They are discussing only theoretical logical worlds, and they write: 'The actual world – this familiar world of ours – is (presumably) a standard one which is (hopefully) devoid of inconsistencies.' But this is precisely what I wonder about. Their inconsistent logical world is the union of two worlds, each in itself consistent. Now suppose that something similar holds where the world of absolute eternal reality intersects the world of our contingent temporal reality. Is it possible that there are logical 'singularities' at points where the timeless reality of God is involved in God's world of time? May it be that the proposition 'God does not suffer' is true *and* the proposition 'God suffers' (not merely in the human nature of Christ) is also true? I would say that here mystery is not only something that is beyond human concepts but also beyond normal human logic.

Nicholas of Cusa (1401–64) thought that we must say that in God there is *coincidentia oppositorum* (literally, a falling together of opposites). He was convinced that, when we speak about God, we are always going to be faced with paradox. His case is not weakened by his use of some quaint and unpersuasive analogies from the infinite in geometry. However, from what I know of his writings, I think that, when he spoke of 'opposites', he usually had in mind contrary terms such as necessary/impossible, rather than contradictory statements such as God suffers/God does not suffer. In these last two chapters I have been suggesting that we have a sort of compound *coincidentia oppositorum*: a loving God who causes suffering in humanity, an impassible God who suffers for and with humanity.

*

I turn now to another aspect of the mystery. The cross is where human evil and human suffering, God's love and God's suffering, come together in all their mystery. That deep mystery is made sacramentally present to us in the celebration of the Eucharist. The Eucharist is sacrifice, adoration, thanksgiving; it is communion with God and his people in a memorial meal; but in the perspective of the last three chapters the aspect that I want to emphasize is that we are involved in the sacramental coming together of sin and suffering and self-giving divine love. (And yet how often at this moment our minds are filled with trivial distractions.)

The Eucharist is both the memorial and the making present of the moment when 'God in Christ was reconciling the world to himself' and when 'God made the sinless one into sin, so that in him we might become the goodness of God' (2 Corinthians 5:19–21). Everything comes together in the figure on the cross. There is all the evil of human history that put him there, and his identification with that evil. (In Chapter 7 I have reflected on the appalling burden it must have been to bear the weight of the sin of the world when he was 'made into sin'.) There is the divine love that is ready to suffer; and there is Jesus' cry of abandonment, which identifies him with all those throughout history who have felt themselves abandoned by God.

As Jung pointed out, the real answer to Job in his suffering was not the overpowering voice of Yahweh from out of the tempest, but the cry of desolation wrung from the Word as he hung on the cross. The answer was not an explanation but an assurance that God is in loving solidarity with sinful and suffering humanity. Jesus, however, was not only the 'image of the invisible God'. 'Behold the man,' said Pilate. Behold what it is to be truly human, he might unwittingly have been saying, as he showed the crowd the scourged figure wearing the crown of thorns. The cross does not explain love; it shows what love, both divine and human, is like. We can only learn what the God of love is like, and at the same time become fully human ourselves, by being disciples of Jesus and following him on the way of the cross.

'He who knows the mystery of the Cross and the Tomb knows too the essential principles of all things.' The Greek theologian St Maximus (d. 662) was right to see the cross of Christ as the key to the understanding of reality. 'He who *knows* the mystery of the Cross': there's the rub. We understand so little of that coming together of evil and suffering and love and redemption. We see only glimpses of the meaning of the mystery of the tree which is an inescapable part of reality:

> . . . The tree,
> with its roots in the mind's dark,
> was divinely planted, the original fork
> in existence.
>
> (R.S. Thomas: 'Amen')

Here the tree of the cross merges with another tree, the mythic tree of good and evil, 'the original fork/in existence'. There is a hint, emphasized by the ambiguity of 'planted', that God bears some responsibility for humankind's choice of evil. At a first reading the next lines of the poem might suggest divine perversity:

> . . . There is no meaning in life,
> unless men can be found to reject
> love. God needs his martyrdom.

By his choice of language Thomas shocks us into meditating anew on the dark enigmas of existence. He makes us ponder the mysteries of 'original sin', and of the paradox that human evil was required to bring the Son of God to the cross whence he redeemed humanity from evil, and of Love's welcoming ('Amen') the inevitability of suffering for his people.

But the cry from the cross is not the last word. St Maximus continues: 'He who penetrates yet further and finds himself initiated into the mystery of the Resurrection apprehends the end for which God created all things.' From the cross God brings forth new life, life whose consummation is union with the Love which Dante saw as the centre of reality and the ground of all being. The first Christians learned to believe the good news that one who had died the degrading death of a criminal was alive with divine life which was his gift to be shared by them. That life comes to us because God the Son took our humanity to himself. As he is for ever united to us, taking our sinfulness upon himself, so we are united to him in his death and resurrection. Human evil was both the cause of the cross and redeemed by the cross. The divine love of Christ has conquered sin in principle; but each of us has to allow him to work this transformation in our lives. 'I have been crucified with Christ, and I live now not with my own life but with the life of Christ who lives in me' (Galatians 2:19–20). This is one of the most frequent Pauline themes: in baptism we have died to sin with Christ and with him we have been born to a new life, begun already in this world and to reach its fullness in the next. In his passionate words to the Corinthians St Paul expresses the essence of the Christian paradox:

> The language of the cross is folly to those who are doomed, but to us who are being saved it is the power of God . . . We preach a crucified Christ; a stumbling-block to Jews and folly to pagans, but to those who have been called . . . Christ the power of God and the wisdom of God. For God's foolishness is wiser than men, and God's weakness is stronger than men. (1 Corinthians 1:18–25)

It is difficult to make this idea of a new life in Christ vitally real in our daily lives. Moreover, Christians too have to struggle to make some sense of the mystery of the evil and the suffering that is in our world; but even as we struggle with this and with trying to understand something of God's response revealed to us from the cross, we have Love's assurance to Julian of Norwich (d. c. 1416):

> I desired oftentimes to witten what was our Lord's meaning. And fifteen years after, and more, I was answered in ghostly understanding, saying thus: 'Wouldst thou

witten thy Lord's meaning in this thing? Wit it well: Love was his meaning. Who shewed it thee? Love. What shewed he thee? Love. Wherefore shewed it he? For Love. Hold thee therein and thou shalt witten and know more in the same. But thou shalt never know nor witten therein other thing. . . .' Thus was I learned that Love was our Lord's meaning. And I saw full surely in this and in all, that ere God made us he loved us; which love was never slacked, nor ever shall be. And in this love he hath done all his works; and in this love he hath made all things profitable to us; and in this love our life is everlasting. In our making we had beginning; but the love wherein he made us was in him from without beginning: in which love we have our beginning. And all this shall we see in God, without end. (Conclusion of *Revelations of Divine Love*)

# 9

# Reality

'Be still, and know that I am God . . .'

Psalm 46:10 (45:10)

ANTHONY DE MELLO devotes the first third of *Sadhana*, his book on prayer, to 'awareness exercises'. He begins with a recommendation to practise periods of silence, trying to attain a silence of heart and mind. Not an easy thing to do, and perhaps more difficult than ever in our contemporary Western world; but some degree of inner silence is necessary as a basis for the exercises in awareness. The first of these is to become aware of the sensations in one's own body: the touch of one's clothes, the pressure of the chair on one's back, the feelings in the skin of face or hands. Among a number of such exercises an important one is to become aware of one's breathing: simply aware for ten or fifteen minutes of the air passing through the nostrils.

The important thing, de Mello says, is not to *think about* what one is feeling, but to concentrate on actually *experiencing* the sensations. He maintains that most people live too much 'in their heads', thinking and imagining, too little conscious of the experience of their senses; and that, as a result, they tend to live in the past or the future, not in the present, which is, after all, the only reality. Getting in touch with sensations in various parts of the body sharpens awareness and also induces a certain stillness in the body, which is a correlative to the quietening of the mind and imagination that is the prerequisite of prayer.

If we take prayer to be the experience of God, then these awareness exercises are already a beginning of prayer. Through them we become directly conscious of some small part of reality, and God is the Ground of all reality. This beginning of an awareness of God can be made more explicit and more overtly religious. For instance, in the breathing exercise we can be conscious of the presence of God's Spirit as we breathe in; and we can experience the sensations in our bodies as the result of biochemical reactions which are God's power at work. There are more profound ways of experiencing God, even for one who is not in any sense a mystic; but the consciousness of the sensations in our bodies is already an experience of God working in us in present reality.

De Mello's exercises are designed to arouse an attentiveness to reality, however humble. This attentiveness is a quality required by scientist, poet and artist, as well as by one seeking to pray. The child is full of wonder at so much that it sees. Happy the adult who has not lost this sense of wonder. We grow so used to all the things around us that most of the time we do not really notice them. The faculty of attentiveness helps to keep us aware of the wonder and the mystery of all reality. Leaving aside the enigmas of our specifically human experience, there is so much in the material world that is both fascinating and paradoxical.

All matter is spread through the universe; yet it is bonded together in what we perceive as objects that are each separate and unique. It was this uniqueness and individuality of every object in the universe that gave such delight to Gerard Manley Hopkins. There is a story that when he was a Jesuit scholastic at Stonyhurst, the gardener found him one day walking round and round one spot on a gravel path. The reason for his apparently bizarre behaviour was that he was gazing intently from every angle at a single pebble in all its individuality. During his philosophy course he was enthralled when he came upon Duns Scotus' concept of *haecceitas*, the 'thisness' of everything, its principle of individuation. The theory of the medieval Franciscan philosopher ('of realty the rarest-veined unraveller', as Hopkins calls him in 'Duns Scotus's Oxford') chimed in completely with the poet's own deeply felt view of material reality. On the matter of attentiveness, Hopkins once wrote in his journal: 'When you look at things hard, they seem to look hard back at you.'

A more rarefied aspect of reality is to be found in mathematics, but here too we find paradox. Most people think that, if anything is certain, it is mathematics; but mathematicians have had some nasty shocks in the last one hundred and fifty years. First came the realization that Euclid's was not the only possible geometry; then that his much admired *Elements* was by no means the supreme model of logical deduction of theorems from axioms, which it had been thought to be for two thousand years. In his proofs Euclid had used many intuitive ideas which were not logically justified from his axioms. In the latter part of the nineteenth century a number of mathematicians addressed the task of putting all of mathematics, not just geometry, on a strict logical basis. Gottlob Frege hoped to do that in his *Fundamental Laws of Arithmetic*, but as the second volume was going to press, he received a letter from the young Bertrand Russell pointing out that one of his concepts led to a contradiction. At the close of Volume II, Frege wrote: 'A scientist can hardly meet with anything more undesirable than to have the foundation give way just as the work is finished. A letter from Mr Russell has put me in this position.' Poor Frege, that 'undesirable' seems a wistful understatement after his years of labour. Russell himself, in collaboration with A.N. Whitehead, tried to do the same as Frege in the three volumes of *Principia Mathematica*. It was a monumental work, but it did not fully achieve their aims. In order to avoid known paradoxes, they had to introduce axioms that were not accepted by many mathematicians. The confident attempt to put mathematics on an impeccable basis of logical deduction continued until a devastating blow was delivered in 1931 by a young Austrian, Kurt Gödel. Roughly speaking, Gödel proved that no substantial branch of mathematics, not even the arithmetic of whole numbers, could be given a fully logical development. He showed that in any such system there would always be propositions whose truth could neither be proved nor disproved. Moreover, he also proved that it is impossible to establish the logical consistency of much of mathematics. In other words, there can never be any absolute guarantee of freedom from paradox and contradiction. Russell gradually came to accept the impossibility of achieving what he and Whitehead had set out to do in the early years of this century; and in 1959 towards the end of his life, he admitted: 'The splendid certainty that I had always hoped to find in mathematics was lost in a bewildering maze.'

If that is the situation in the world of mathematics, it is not surprising that we keep meeting the strange, the inexplicable, the paradoxical in more substantial areas of reality, whether it be in the perplexing consequences of quantum theory or the complexities of the human heart or the relationship of God to his creatures. Reality is like a slashed football which cannot be made to lie flat. Push down one part and another rises up. Not seldom it is difficult to see how two assertions can be reconciled to each other, though both seem to be valid. 'The last step of reason is to recognise that there are an infinity of things that are beyond it. It is merely feeble if it does not go so far as to grasp that' (Pascal, *Pensées* B267).

It is above all in questions relating to God that reason is so insufficient. It seems incomprehensible that God exists, and incomprehensible that he doesn't, incomprehensible that God suffers and that he doesn't. If I try to reflect using my imagination, I find many things relating to God completely beyond my grasp. It is, for instance, impossible to have any sort of realistic picture of what life after death might be like. Then there are more philosophical problems, as, for instance: if God is Absolute Being, there cannot exist anything outside or separate from him, and yet the universe cannot be a part of God. Despite all this, Christians retain a firm conviction. They believe, of course, that this is a gift from God, the gift of faith. Nevertheless, faith does not exist apart from human considerations which support belief. I think many find that a number of such considerations converge, as it were, towards the conviction that their God-given faith does in fact – despite all the deep puzzlement and inexplicable elements – provide the best 'fit' to their experience of reality. For those who have this faith an important element can be the experience that comes from prayer. And so we come back to the purpose lying behind Anthony de Mello's awareness exercises.

As I have said, these exercises in awareness of aspects of physical reality can be an introduction to awareness of God, the Absolute Reality behind all contingent reality; and this is the beginning of contemplative prayer. This last phrase can seem rather frightening, suggesting some deep mystical experience beyond the reach of most of us; but I am using it simply to make a distinction between this and verbal or liturgical prayer. It refers to the prayer which is, however dimly, a direct non-conceptual awareness of God. This first stage can lead both inwards and outwards. It leads us inwards into our emptiness, to the sharp experience of contingency, as for Sartre's Roquentin, though for him this did not lead to God but only to absurdity. In this kind of prayer we have a profound experience, not just of our createdness, but of our creaturehood, of our total dependence on God as the Ground of our being. God is not 'out there'; he is at the very centre of our emptiness, as St John of the Cross emphasized so often. In prayer this conviction of our complete dependence on God is not the conclusion of any reasoning process but an experience of our whole being. This kind of prayer is a matter of 'just being conscious'. It is the nearest we get to just 'being', neither doing nor thinking. It is analogous to the silent consciousness of a mother beside her sleeping child or of lovers in each other's arms.

There is a widespread contemporary fear of silence because it can lead a person to be faced by their inner emptiness. Many of Samuel Beckett's characters exhibit this fear when they talk aimlessly to cover over the abyss of nothingness, even though the talk is pointless and the whole exercise therefore absurd. But in fact silence provides the conditions that can reveal reality, from the reality of our bodily sensations to that of our existential emptiness and the presence of God; and the going inwards in prayer also makes one more self-aware. In God's presence we become more aware of the good and the evil that is in us. Prayer is the place where it is most difficult to hide from ourselves. Although we experience our weakness and poverty in our failures in daily life, in our dealings with others and in moral action, it is perhaps only in the emptiness of prayer that we are faced with our total and radical poverty. Without God we are nothing. But paradoxically, the emptiness which we experience in prayer is also the beginning of the fullness of being for which we are destined in the final union with our Creator. The self-awareness that is the consequence of prayer is not introversion, and it certainly does not give any boost to the ego-self. Moreover, it is only a by-product of prayer, because at a deeper level contact with God is only possible if self-consciousness is transcended.

God is not another being over against our being, although it is very difficult to say anything about God that does not make it sound like that. We cannot grasp how it is that we are neither separate from God nor part of God. He is the Ground of our being, and so is at the centre of our true Self. In his commentary on 'The Living Flame of Love', St John of the Cross goes so far as to say that the soul's centre *is* God. What I have called Dante's Way to the Centre is not a journey outwards but inwards to the God who is the centre of every self, as he is of all reality. Whatever precisely Empedocles had in mind so many centuries ago, he has left us a suggestive idea in his 'God is a circle whose centre is everywhere and whose circumference is nowhere'. I have mentioned Dante's poetic vision of God as a point of light around which all creation revolves. About sixty years later, in 1373, Julian of Norwich had an actual imaginative vision: 'After this I saw God in a point, that is to say, in my understanding, by which sight I saw that he is in all things' (*Revelations*, chapter 11).

This account of the relationship in prayer between the true Self and God can make it sound impersonal, but that is far from the case. The difficulty is that our experience of God is unique and cannot easily be expressed. A John of the Cross, who has emptied out the ego-self and is thus conscious of the God who fills him, can burst into incandescent poetry; but for most of us it is much more prosaic, because it is not usually felt in any ordinary sense. It *is*, in Martin Buber's terms, an I-Thou relationship; but this is not an adequate description, since it implies two subjects. God is not outside us, and so in truth the relationship is closer than the personal relationship of two humans who love each other. God is *in* our very person, so the relationship is transpersonal, *beyond* the personal, even though we do not experience it in the same way that we do human relationships. It is significant that in both the illustrative comparisons to contemplative prayer which I gave earlier (mother and sleeping child, two lovers), the silent bond in the relationship was that of love. For the Christian, it all comes a little closer to ordinary human experience through faith in Jesus Christ as God incarnate and our Redeemer. Absent though he is in the flesh, his life and words and what he has done for us give human warmth to prayer.

In yet another paradox, the movement inwards in prayer can lead to a movement outwards. Attentiveness to God within the self leads to attentiveness to all his creation, to the needs of the human world and to a consciousness of our share of responsibility. It is significant that contemplative monks and nuns have been a notable presence in the contemporary concern about justice and peace in the world. We are all responsible for each other because the human race is a unity. I believe that this unity is to be understood in a strong sense and not as arising merely from the abstract idea of a 'common humanity'. Just as all matter is interconnected, so I believe that all spirit is interconnected, not in the separateness of the ego-selves, but in the true Self of each, one with all others in the Ground of their being, who is God. The mystery is that in both the physical and the spiritual there is nevertheless such a wonderful diversity. Each material thing and each person has such precious individuality. In human beings the true Self lies deeper than the personality, which can in some cases be so drastically altered by physical causes. In virtue of the incarnation and redemption, the spirit at the centre of the Self is the divine Spirit of Christ, outwardly manifested in the wonderful variety of human persons. Hopkins expresses his cherished concept of the unique individuality of every being, both the purely material and the human, in a sonnet in which he emphasizes that this individuality is chiefly manifested in activity:

As kingfishers catch fire, dragonflies draw flame;
  As tumbled over rim in roundy wells
  Stones ring; like each tucked string tells, each hung bell's
Bow swung finds tongue to fling out broad its name;
Each mortal thing does one thing and the same:
  Deals out that being indoors each one dwells;

Selves – goes itself; *myself* it speaks and spells,
Crying *What I do is me: for that I came.*

I say more: the just man justices;
Keeps gráce: thát keeps all his goings graces;
Acts in God's eye what in God's eye he is –
Chríst. For Christ plays in ten thousand places,
Lovely in limbs, and lovely in eyes not his
To the Father through the features of men's faces.

In time of prayer we can also think of ourselves as the spiritual consciousness of all creation. In adoration we give expression to the glory that all things give to God. So Henry Vaughan in 'The Morning Watch':

The rising winds,
And falling springs,
Birds, beasts, all things
Adore him in their kinds.
Thus all is hurl'd
In sacred Hymnes, and Order, The great Chime
And Symphony of nature. *Prayer is*
*The world in tune.*

If in prayer we can be the spiritual 'representatives' before God of the whole of material creation, how much more important is it to remember to be present in prayer with those who cannot pray, because they do not know how to, or are too busy, or are in too great distress. We can join ourselves in prayer with the sick and the dying and the lonely and the imprisoned.

*

One of the deepest of all paradoxes is that, while God is 'more near to me than I am to myself', as St Augustine said, he is also the totally Other. Human beings have always had a sense of the numinous which arouses a feeling of awe, well described by Wordsworth in *The Prelude*. This is not necessarily connected with any specifically religious conviction; it may be a half-formed recognition of a *mysterium tremendum*, majestic and transcending quotidian human activity. When it occurs within a theistic tradition, it is the awe experienced in face of the majesty of God, as in Isaiah's vision of his call, when the seraphim cried out: 'Holy, holy, holy is the Lord God of Hosts' (6:3). Holiness in this context does not connote moral perfection; it is that mysterious and majestic reality outside the human person which evokes a sense of awe and solemn wonder in a way which is not conceptual. At this first moment of the experience of the Totally Other, the Transcendent, the ethical element does not yet enter. But there follows a second moment when the majesty of the numinous inspires a feeling of unworthiness in the subject, as in Isaiah's reaction to his vision: 'What a wretched state I am in! I am lost, for I am a man of unclean lips . . . and my eyes have looked at the King, the God of Hosts'. This recognition of God's holiness leads to adoration, the proper stance of the creature before its Creator; and it is right that adoration should have a predominant part in our prayer.

In the Western world there certainly seems to have been a loss of the sense of the numinous in recent times. There is a tendency in our culture to be concerned only with verifiable factual knowledge, and there is also a desire to be in control, in control of one's life and the world around. So there is talk of the human race having 'reached maturity' and having 'grown out of the naïveté' of believing in the transcendent. This is not very convincing. The history of our times gives little support to the contention that human beings are now more mature than their forebears. There is also the contemporary obsession with 'image'. Public figures and ordinary people are concerned with the image that they project, not with the reality that they are. Politicians and businessmen and women talk about 'living in the real world', when they mean that they are acting from expediency not from principle. The claim that reality does not include anything transcending the human is not impressive. It may well be true that the sort of personalities produced by modern technological society have great difficulty in being aware of the transcendent. This may well be a factor in the lack of psychological health in the contemporary West.

The intuition of the transcendent has often led to the setting aside of persons, objects and places to be dedicated to the sacred; and to them has been attributed an apartness that corresponds to the experience of the holiness of the transcendent Other. I believe that this remains a sound instinct, especially as regards buildings dedicated to worship. There is, however, a danger of regarding the sacred and the profane as two realities. There are not two realities, but two depths (or rather two perceptions) of the one only reality. Human beings have within them the capacity to sense the numinous in the reality which they experience. The Christian outlook is to think, not so much in terms of sacred persons, objects or places, but rather of sacred moments in which there is a conjunction of all three, as in the celebration of the Eucharist. This moment can be experienced equally at a baroque High Mass in a great church and at a Eucharist celebrated in the home at an undecorated table and without special vestments. In the celebration of any of the sacraments, the Christian is not moving from a secular plane to a sacred one. The sacraments are signs of the dimension of the holy which in fact is always present in so-called secular existence. They are symbols of that dimension of reality which lies unrecognized for much of the time. The resolution of the mistaken antithesis between sacred and profane is most clearly seen in the person of Christ. At the incarnation God entered human history once and for all. It is interesting that in the Eastern Christian tradition, Christ's transfiguration on Mount Tabor is not seen as a moment when he allowed his divinity to shine through his humanity, but as a moment when the three apostles became aware of the reality of the glory of God which was in fact always present in the human reality. Christ on earth was the sacrament of God, the sign of the All Holy present in secular reality. By a divine paradox the supreme moment of that theophany came on Golgotha, the central moment of all history.

*

A difficulty in writing anything about prayer is the great discrepancy between what is said and what is the actual conscious experience. Most of prayer time seems to be idled away, with the imagination and memory running rampant, the mind unengaged. One feels that one has never learned to pray. Nothing seems to happen. And all the time God remains silent. Nevertheless, over the years comes the realization that prayer *has* had an effect. It modifies our outlook on life and our awareness of the depths of reality. Despite boredom and the frequent waiting for the period of prayer to end, we discover that we would miss it. For those who have experienced prayer, it is integral to the rest of life and gives it meaning. Our lives need times of prayer; and just as the individual needs to set aside some part of daily life, so the world needs lives that are set aside for prayer. So it is good that there should be religious communities leading lives devoted primarily to contemplative prayer.

We may be far from the mystic's 'dark knowledge of God', but our feeling of emptiness in prayer is not unrelated to it. It is a good experience, because it corresponds to the reality of our existential emptiness and total dependence on God. Despite all distractions, we try to wait attentively in silence upon God, the only Absolute Reality. We are scarcely aware of the experience because it lies below the level of feeling or concept. Perhaps it can best be described by an oxymoron: prayer is an unfelt experience.

When St Thomas says that we cannot know what God is, only what God is not, he is referring to rational thought and discourse *about* God. There is, however, a knowledge *of* God which is a direct awareness of him, however dim, in the depth of our being. Here we have the paradox of knowing the Unknowable. This is a kind of knowledge that can lead to love but not to thought, as the author of *The Cloud of Unknowing* insists: 'Of God himself can no man think . . . he may well be loved, but not thought. By love may he be gotten and holden, but by thought neither.' He says that although it is good sometimes to *think* about the kindness and goodness of God, that is not of the essence, which is to try to pierce the darkness with love: 'Smite upon that thick cloud of unknowing with a sharp dart of longing love' (chapter 6).

The experience of God, though so dark and hidden and sometimes seemingly obliterated, lies deeper even than the mind's acceptance of the laws of logic. It is not surprising that we are met by paradox when we try to speak about the One about whom we cannot speak. Mathematicians now know that absolute certainty can never be achieved in the foundations of their subject, and yet, built upon those foundations, there is an immense and ever growing superstructure of pure mathematics about whose validity they do not doubt. Nor is it really clear why abstract mathematics can provide such good and fruitful models for the physical world. The applied mathematician and the physicist make an act of faith that is certainly justified by the amazing achievements of modern physics and cosmology. How much more is an act of faith necessary in everything that concerns that Reality which is beyond all sense experience and all purely rational thought; but it is a faith supported by an experience, however fragmentary, of the God who is both at the centre of our being and the totally Other. Below our puzzled anguish about suffering and evil, we are aware in prayer of the immanence and the transcendence of Ultimate Reality, silent in the depths of the Abyss, but revealed as Love, above all in the life, death and resurrection of Jesus Christ.

# 10

# A Very Rich Poor Man

Ditissimus pauper
Thomas of Celano: *Life of St Francis*

When the first biographer of St Francis of Assisi, Thomas of Celano, called him a very rich poor man, he had found a neat phrase to sum up one of the greatest followers of Jesus Christ. St Francis is a supreme example of the integration of the negative and the positive in the Christian way to God.

Born in Assisi in 1182, the son of a wealthy cloth-merchant and of a mother who may have been French or Provençal, he was baptized Giovanni; but his father, who travelled frequently to France on business, called him Francesco, the little Frenchman. He became the leader of the pleasure-loving youth of Assisi; but he was generous-hearted and full of the ideals of knightly chivalry. When he was twenty-one, Assisi went to war against the neighbouring city of Perugia. The Assisans were defeated; Francis was taken prisoner, spent nearly a year in a Perugian dungeon, and suffered a serious illness as a result of his imprisonment. This harsh experience proved to be the beginning of a profound transformation in the young man. He lost his taste for his former frivolous way of life, and he began to spend time alone in prayer, as well as becoming even more generous to the poor. One day on his way home he saw to his horror a leper approaching him. Francis, who was by temperament extremely fastidious, overcame his repugnance and kissed the leper's stump of a hand. Not long afterwards, as he was praying in the church of San Damiano near Assisi, he seemed to hear the figure of Christ on the crucifix say to him, 'Repair my house which you see is falling down'. At the time, he took this literally, and sold a bale of his father's cloth to pay for repairing San Damiano. Not unnaturally, his father was extremely angry; less justifiably, he had his son arraigned before the bishop's court. In a characteristically dramatic gesture, Francis not only repaid the money but took off the rich clothes which he had resumed for the occasion, threw them at his father's feet, and, clothed only in a hair shirt, declared that he now had only one Father, who was in heaven.

Francis was now twenty-five years old. He laboured on the repairing of the church of San Damiano, visited lepers and lived on the scraps of food which he begged. At first he was mocked when he appeared in Assisi, begging and dressed in tatters; but, preaching about the love of God there and in other Umbrian towns, he soon gathered a group of followers. In 1210 he and eleven companions went to Rome to obtain the authorization of Pope Innocent III to lead a life of total poverty as roving preachers. They lived in wattle huts around the Portiuncula chapel in the plain below Assisi, and went out preaching in pairs. The number of these *frati minori*, 'lesser brothers', as Francis called them, grew rapidly throughout Italy. Here was a new kind of religious life, quite unlike the ordered, stable monastic life which had been the norm until then. There was a minimum of organization, and the ideal of poverty included the refusal of even corporate ownership. In 1212 St Francis founded with St Clare the first community of nuns, though even he had to accept the then universal tradition that nuns must live in enclosed convents.

Within a very few years, the number of friars had grown so great throughout Europe that some kind of organization became a necessity. This gave rise to tensions, because Francis himself and most of his first companions wished to preserve the initial inspiration of a life of total poverty and of evangelical freedom, without books or human learning; but not all agreed. In 1221 St Francis wrote a revised version of his simple rule, but it had to be modified to be acceptable to all. He suffered a great deal in his last years because he felt that his ideal was being lost. In 1224 while he was praying on Monte La Verna, high in the Apennines, he received the stigmata of the five wounds of Christ, which remained visible in his body until his death two years later. During his last years he also suffered great physical pain. He became so weak that, much against his will, he had to allow himself to be put on a donkey to make journeys, as he could no longer walk. He was now virtually blind, and he underwent the agonizing and useless medieval remedy of cauterization. He died at his beloved Portiuncula in 1226 at the age of forty-four, asking that his body should be laid naked on the ground, to signify his desire for total poverty in imitation of his Saviour.

By the time of his death, Francis' fame was so widespread and his sanctity so manifest ('a man drunk with the love of God,' one chronicler said) that he was canonized within two years of his death; and in that same year of 1228 there began the building of the magnificent basilica to house the body of the *poverello*, the little poor man, who had insisted that his followers should possess neither property nor buildings. There will be more to be said in due course about the irony of that.

One obvious reason for the popularity of St Francis of Assisi in the modern world is the attractiveness of his personality. The legends about his preaching to the birds and the taming of the wolf of Gubbio, and the way he went about singing the praises of the Creator, show his responsiveness to the natural world and his love of beauty. A radiant joy seemed to emanate from him and his early companions. He himself called his little company *joculatores Domini*, the Lord's minstrels. It is this outgoing warmth, this love of all God's creatures, this joy, which endear him to so many, even those who do not share his faith. All this is valid enough. St Francis is a wonderful example of the positive way to God, the *via affirmativa*, the way that leads from appreciation and love of this world to love of its Creator.

This is, however, only part of the truth about St Francis; and many who admire him for these romantic, even sentimental, reasons would be repelled by another facet of his personality: his frightening asceticism. He treated his body with extreme harshness, calling it 'the enemy'. It was only in the last months of his life that he was persuaded to relent a little, when he realized that he had been excessively hard on his body, which after all was also a part of God's creation. He then apologized to Brother Ass for maltreating him. He insisted on his followers living in absolute poverty, owning nothing even corporately. He had an obsessive hatred of money, which he described as excrement. The brothers were to work or, if necessary, to beg for their food, but never to accept money to buy it. He even considered that true poverty required the renunciation of human learning. This insistence on absolute poverty was based on the dubious foundation of a conviction that Christ and his apostles had lived without ownership of any sort, so that, as he saw it, imitation of Christ required such poverty. Any contravention of his rules about poverty was liable to be met with an explosive outburst of anger, as when Francis found that the brothers had built in stone a house of studies at the University of Bologna. In his eyes this offended against that abandonment of both property and learning, which he regarded as essential to true poverty.

St Francis was a more complex person than the simple *poverello* of popular tradition. There was indeed a great simplicity about him in the sense that his convictions and his reactions had an absolute quality; but some of these can seem disconcerting to us today. In his youth he had been something of an exhibitionist, and he remained a man of extravagant gesture, as when he threw all his clothes at his father's feet in the bishop's palace, or when he commanded Bernard to trample on him as a punishment for some supposed proud thought. His gestures, however, were always truly symbolic. His dying request to be laid naked on the ground was intended both as an imitation of Christ's nakedness on the cross and as an expression of the human race's union with the whole material creation. His acting out of the Nativity scene with living figures proved to be the beginning of the popularization of the Christmas crib. He was a man of immense gentleness, courtesy and compassion, who could yet have outbursts of burning anger, especially when he considered that his ideals of poverty were being infringed.

The surroundings of his native city can stand as a symbol of the man. Assisi looks down on the lovely soft Umbrian countryside, while to the east rises the forbidding presence of bare, rocky Monte Subasio. St Francis was gifted with an immense store of affectivity; and he saw that, precisely for this reason, it needed to be disciplined by a fierce asceticism. In this way he achieved the integration of the positive and negative sides of his rich temperament. I think one small incident illustrates much of what was in St Francis. One day when he was travelling the roads on a preaching mission with a companion, he picked up two sticks, placed one between chin and shoulder and used the other as a mock fiddle-bow in a typical piece of childlike buffoonery. Then he suddenly burst into tears. The crossed sticks had brought to his mind the sufferings of his beloved Saviour on the cross and his own sins that had contributed to them; but they were at the same time happy tears at the thought of God's tender and forgiving mercy.

I think that there is also a deeper, if less generally recognized, reason for the popularity of St Francis. All human beings thirst for freedom. Many think that they will find it if they can bring about material circumstances that will allow them to act as they desire. But true freedom does not lie there. Whether we recognize it or not, we long, not just for such external freedom, but for a fundamental inner freedom. We long to be free of fears and inhibitions, not to be constrained by our desires, to rise above the accidents of life so that our happiness does not depend on circumstances. This is the true freedom that is characteristic of so many of the saints. We see it, for instance, in St Teresa of Avila. She spent herself in founding convents of the Reformed Carmelites all over Spain and fought hard for the success of this work; but she was perfectly content to accept the possibility that all this labour should come to nothing.

It is a freedom that springs, not from apathy, but from a sort of positive detachment, a total liberty of spirit. St Francis of Assisi is a superlative example of a human being with that total inner freedom that all people dream of, consciously or unconsciously. He possessed to the highest degree a passionate love for all things created and a complete detachment from them. I remember a Franciscan retreat-giver many years ago speaking glowingly of the beauties of nature and then saying that one should from time to time turn away from them, because this was the only way both to preserve one's freedom and to love them truly for their own sake. Here was the true Franciscan spirit.

In his book *I Francis*, Carlo Caretto makes Francis say: 'My illness during my captivity in Perugia did two great things for me. It deprived me of my security, and it gave me new eyes'. Having experienced the deprivations of imprisonment and grave illness in a dungeon, he came to have an even greater appreciation of the visible world. He also learned that freedom did not depend on material security. Francis and his early companions achieved a supremely joyful freedom without any permanent buildings to live in nor source of food beyond what they worked for or begged. So Caretto's Francis says again: 'We had solved the problem that most vexes and preoccupies human beings: the problem of tomorrow.' This living in the perfect love that casts out fear is at the heart of St Francis' great and continuing attraction.

The fullness of joy through radical detachment permeates the stories about St Francis and his first companions in the *Fioretti* (*The Little Flowers of St Francis*), which are so redolent of the early Franciscan spirit. But this joy is not something easily achieved by ignoring the harsh realities of life, as is made clear in one of the most famous incidents in the *Fioretti*. One bitterly cold winter's day when returning with Brother Leo from Perugia to the Portiuncula outside Assisi, Francis tells Leo that perfect joy does not consist in having great gifts of learning or of eloquence or for working miracles. He says that when they reach the Portiuncula, drenched by rain, numb with cold and tormented with hunger, the porter will answer the door. If he says that they are a pair of scoundrels and refuses to let them in, leaving them standing and shivering in the snow; and if, despite their repeated knocking, he beats them and chases them away, then, says Francis: 'if we accept all that with humility, patience and charity, Brother Leo, write that therein consists perfect joy'.

The stories forming the *Fioretti* were gathered together about a hundred years after the death of St Francis. They are mostly based on actual events, turned into symbols of spiritual reality. The authors were wanting to give a living picture of a person and of his influence. There is something unique about the stories in the *Fioretti*: a simplicity that appears naïve, a love for all human beings and for all creation, a holy joy that breaks out in seemingly bizarre manifestations, a liberty of spirit unencumbered by worldly cares and desires. This is truly the spirit of St Francis. The atmosphere is well captured in Rossellini's film *Francesco, Giullare di Dio* (*Francis, God's Jester*, 1950). The film is made up of individual episodes from the *Fioretti*, each prefaced by the words on screen of the relevant chapter heading. As so often, Rossellini used non-professional actors; and this time they were real Franciscan friars. He managed to convey visually the 'divine madness' of Francis and his early companions.

The freedom of which I have been speaking, so evident in St Francis, had its foundation in radical poverty. From the moment he renounced all worldly goods in front of his father and the bishop, poverty became, not something negative, but a positive good to be sought. 'No man has ever had as strong a passion for gold as Francis had for poverty,' wrote St Bonaventure in his life of St Francis. It was the pearl of great price. Francis came to speak of poverty in the language of medieval romance as a great lady, whom he and his companions must serve faithfully. As I have said, he became almost obsessive in his hatred of money, whose very touch he felt would befoul the friars. Failure in poverty was the only thing that made him severe as a superior. Poverty was the foundation of the spiritual life, so that humility and simplicity were seen as expressions of poverty of spirit. This poverty of spirit sprang from Francis' burning love for Christ. Christ had lived, so he thought, in absolute poverty and he died in naked poverty on the cross. The only way to imitate Christ fully was to follow him in equal poverty. It was also a way of making oneself totally dependent on God. As Thomas of Celano reports, when St Francis lay dying, he 'rejoiced greatly and his heart was gladdened when he saw that he had been faithful to Lady Poverty to the end' (*Second Life* II 162).

When we read of the extremes of poverty deliberately sought by Francis and his first companions, we may feel some distaste for their absoluteness or else a slight embarrassment at our own comfortable lives; but the fact remains that this gave them a remarkable freedom, peace and light-hearted joyousness. These words to his followers may well give us cause for wry reflection:

'If we have money, we shall also have to have armed men to guard it'. Some fifty years later a Franciscan friar with the same ardent spirit as the founder, the poet Jacopone da Todi, reputed author of the *Stabat mater*, wrote:

Povertà è nulla habere
e nulla cosa poi volere
e omne cosa possidere
en spirito de libertade

*(Poverty is to have nothing, and then to desire nothing, and to possess all things in a spirit of freedom)*

*

Altissimu onnipotente bon Signore,
tue so le laude la gloria e l'honore et omne benedictione,
Ad te solo, Altissimo, se konfano
Et nullu omo ene dignu te mentovare.

Laudato sie, mi Signore, cum tucte le tue creature,
Spetialmente messor lo frate sole
Lo quale jorna et allumini noi per loi;
Et ellu è bellu e radiante cum grande splendore;
de te, Altissimo, porta significatione.

Laudato si', mi Signore, per sora luna e le stelle,
in celu l'ai formate clarite et pretiose et belle.

Laudato si', mi Signore, per frate vento
et per aere et nubilo et sereno et onne tempo,
per lo quale a le tue creature dai sustentamento.

Laudato si', mi Signore, per sora aqua,
la quale è multo utile et humile et pretiosa et casta.

Laudato si', mi Signore, per frate focu
per lo quale annallumini la nocte;
ed ello è bello et jocundo et robustoso et forte.

Laudato si', mi Signore, per sora nostra matre terra,
la quale ne sustenta et governa
et produce diversi fructi con coloriti flori et herba.

*(Most high, almighty, good Lord, yours are the praises, the glory, and the honour and every blessing; to you alone, Most High, do they belong and no man is worthy to mention you.*

*Be praised, my Lord, with all your creatures, especially Sir brother sun who brings day, and you give us light through him; and he is beautiful and radiant with a great splendour; from you, Most High, he takes meaning.*

*Be praised, my Lord, through sister moon and the stars, in heaven you made them clear and precious and beautiful.*

*Be praised, my Lord, through brother wind and through the air and through cloudy and serene and every kind of weather, by which you give sustenance to your creatures.*

*Be praised, my Lord, through sister water who is very useful and humble and precious and pure.*

*Be praised, my Lord, through brother fire through whom you illumine the night; and he is beautiful and joyful and vigorous and strong.*

*Be praised, my Lord, through sister our mother earth, who sustains and rules us and produces different fruits with coloured flowers and grass.)*

St Francis did not compose this great hymn of praise to the Creator in the early light-hearted years of life with his first company of followers, but in 1225, when he was a very sick man, virtually blind, suffering from painful bodily ailments, and suffering also in spirit from the feeling that his original vision was being lost through modifications made to his rule.

Too ill to make a projected journey to Rieti, he lay in a wattle hut in the garden of San Damiano, where St Clare had her convent. A terrible spiritual darkness came upon him for a period; then one day it lifted and he composed the 'Canticle of Brother Sun' and taught his companions to sing it.

The following year, still ill and weak, he heard that the Bishop of Assisi and the *podestà*, or governor, of the town were at loggerheads for political reasons. He added the following verse and sent some of the brothers to sing the Canticle to the bishop and the *podestà*:

Laudato si', mi Signore, per quelli ke perdonano
per lo tuo amore,
et sostengo infirmitate et tribulatione;
beati quelli kei sosterrano in pace,
ka da te, Altissimo, sirano incoronati.

*(Be praised, my Lord, through those who forgive through your love, and bear infirmity and tribulation; blessed are those who will bear in peace, for by you, Most High, they will be crowned.)*

When they heard this song, the two opponents were moved to be reconciled with each other. A few weeks later, knowing that death was near, Francis sent for Leo and Angelo, whom he asked to sing his Canticle once more. When they had finished, he himself added a final verse:

Laudato si', mi Signore, per sora nostra morte corporale
da la quale nullu homo vivente po skappare;
guai a quelli ke morrano ne le peccata mortali,
beati quelli ke trovarà ne le tue sanctissime voluntati
ka la morte secunda nol farrà male.

*(Be praised, my Lord, through sister our bodily death, from whom no living man can escape; woe to those who die in mortal sin,*

*blessed those whom it will find in your most holy will, for the second death will not do them harm.)*

The Canticle, written in the Umbrian form of the vernacular, is one of the earliest extant poems in Italian. Troubadour poetry had reached the peak of its achievement not long before the birth of St Francis and was well known in Italy. Francis was almost certainly familiar with Provençal song, but his own poem shows no resemblance to the sophistication and metrical complexities of the troubadours. It seems to have been composed virtually extempore, and its form is a sort of free verse with assonance. Yet after more than seven hundred years the freshness of its inspiration still comes through to us. It is especially moving that it was a man who could no longer see who was singing of the beauties of the visible world.

Most English versions translate the repeated preposition *per* as 'for', making the Canticle a hymn of gratitude to God for his gifts of creation; but *per* can also mean 'through', and this seems to me to give the deepest meaning and the one most consonant with St Francis' outlook. For him created beings were the means of a two-way movement between God and the human race. He saw creation as revelatory of God. St Bonaventure says: 'He exulted in all the works of the Creator's hands, and, by the beauty of the images, his spirit rose to their origin and cause. He admired supreme beauty in all beautiful things . . . To him all creation was a stairway which led towards him who is the goal of all desires.' And again: 'He taught the brothers to praise God *in* all things and *through* all his creatures.' 'He was wont to call all creatures his brothers and sisters'; in other words, he achieved a sense of the universal brotherhood of nature and the unity of all creation; and so men and women are able to praise God *through* all created things, and, indeed, through all the vicissitudes of human existence on earth. Death itself is our sister, through whom we can give praise to God.

Here St Francis transforms the *via negativa* into a *via affirmativa*.

I have mentioned the irony of the contrast between St Francis' desire to die naked on the bare earth and the fact that within a few years his body lay in the great basilica of Assisi. The man entrusted with the construction of a shrine to house the saint's body was Elias, one of Francis' first companions, a man whose sincere love and reverence for Francis became progressively overshadowed by his grandiose ideas for the order and by his personal ambition, as was to become sadly evident when he was elected Minister General in 1232.

Elias clearly moved right away from the true Franciscan spirit; but a very real problem had already arisen some years before the founder's death because of the rapid increase of the *frati minori*. The original small band of spiritual enthusiasts led a life of great simplicity without permanent buildings or communal possessions; but within a few years their number had increased to perhaps five thousand, spread first throughout Italy and soon over most of Europe. It became necessary to have some sort of organization, as well as corporate ownership at least as regards housing, clothing and prayer-books. This was already true during Francis' last years (and caused him anguish); it became a more acute problem after his death, when the friars were no longer held together by the personality of the saint but had become a 'movement' within the Church.

Some, including most of the original band of companions, were determined to keep to the absolute poverty and simplicity of life of the first years, but others felt that some modification was necessary. Conflict arose between the first group, who came to be known as the Spirituals, and the latter, called the Conventuals. It was inevitable (especially with the authority of the papacy working in that direction) that the original rule should be modified, until a spontaneous movement became a structured 'religious order' integrated into the life of the

Church, not least in the universities, which in the thirteenth century were becoming new centres of learning (and here British Franciscans like Roger Bacon, William of Occam and Duns Scotus played a distinguished part in Oxford and Paris). By the beginning of the fourteenth century some of the Spirituals were in open conflict with the papacy. They held that it was certain that Christ and his apostles had lived in absolute poverty, and that therefore the Church, to be true to its founder, must do likewise. The upholders of this extreme doctrine came to be called *fraticelli*, and, not unexpectedly, were declared heretics by the pope. They, in their turn, pronounced Pope John XXII to be heretical! There followed the inevitable persecution by the Inquisition. All this provides one of the themes for Umberto Eco's *The Name of the Rose* (1983).

These conflicts of the first hundred years of Franciscan history reflect the insoluble dilemma that was already present in St Francis' lifetime. Those of us who are not Franciscans may also feel ambivalent. We may have the greatest admiration for St Francis and his ideal of absolute poverty and the total liberty of spirit which results from that detachment; but can we regret the building within the century of that immense and wonderfully beautiful Franciscan church of Santa Croce in Florence? It is true that both that church at one end of the city and the Dominicans' Santa Maria Novella at the other were regarded as public churches built for the whole commune *ad utilitatem animarum et decorum civitatis* ('for the benefit of souls and the beauty of the city'), in the words of the archival documentation; but St Francis would have been horrified by the magnificence of the building given over to his brethren. And yet it is so beautiful; and in this beauty lifts human spirits towards the divine.

*

'Shining like the dawn and the morning star, like the sun

flooding the earth with ardent streams of light to make it fruitful, thus Francis appeared . . . His words and deeds were like a clear light, resplendent with truth, flaming with love, awakening a new and finer life . . . It was like the coming of Spring to the world.' So begins Giovanni di Ceprano's *Legend of St Francis*, written in the 1240s and based on the memories of Leo and others of the saint's original companions. This describes well the impact of the life of St Francis on the Christendom of his time. The absoluteness of his way of living out the imitation of Christ in total poverty could not survive in everyday life once the number of his followers had made an 'institution' inevitable. It was a dream, which in its first simplicity could not last. Nevertheless, it had a lasting effect. The coming of the friars transformed the life of the Church of the thirteenth century; and the influence of St Francis remains to this day. His words and deeds are 'resplendent with truth, flaming with love,' and they awaken a desire for a 'finer life'. I have suggested that he was a man who lived out the dream of all people for total freedom of spirit, unshackled by either external or internal constraints.

In particular, St Francis shows us how to accept, indeed to welcome, death. He transformed the trauma of death into the supreme expression of freedom. His welcoming of sister death was the culmination of his integration of the *via negativa* with the *via affirmativa*. We shall all, in the end, have to learn to do this.

# 11

# Empty-handed

> 'Naked I came from my mother's womb,
> naked I shall return.
> The Lord gave, the Lord has taken back.
> Blessed be the name of the Lord.'
>
> Job 1:21

AT THE STAGE OF LIFE when you may have, with something like equal probability, ten years to live or ten weeks, you become acutely aware of your contingency. You understand very clearly that not much separates you from your final destiny: either erasure from a meaningless universe or the final stage of the journey to the Centre of which I wrote in Chapter 5. I am one for whom the experience of contingency is one factor in the conviction that there is such a creative Centre; and my Christian belief is that the destiny intended for me by my Creator is union with him. This is not to say that the times when one seems to face obliteration are mere passing moods. A main theme of this book has been that the two deepest levels of human experience are, on the one hand, a sense of a transient existence on the edge of the void, and on the other, some initial hint of our high destiny, which is union with God.

As we move through the later stages of the journey, we find that our physical and mental powers are gradually but inexorably declining. This is not easy to accept, and we may well at times share Yeats' rage:

What shall I do with this absurdity –
O heart, O troubled heart – this caricature,
Decrepit age that has been tied to me
As to a dog's tail?

(from 'The Tower')

All the beauty and the wonder of this world are no longer experienced with such a sharp and passionate intensity as they were in youth. What is left may sometimes seem to be only the dry memory of them:

Ash on an old man's sleeve
Is all the ash the burnt roses leave.

(T.S. Eliot: 'Little Gidding' II)

A little further on in the same poem there are lines reminiscent of Matthew Arnold's in his 'Growing Old':

It is to suffer this,
And feel but half, and feebly, what we feel.
Deep in our hidden heart
Festers the dull remembrance of a change,
But no emotion – none.

In earlier years we took it for granted that the body would work efficiently; now we find that this is no longer the case, nor do the senses respond to the external world with such acute enjoyment. Memory begins to fail us, and we find that our mental grasp is weakening.

It is not surprising that feelings of frustration and resentment may sometimes bubble up when one experiences the losses that come with age; and yet, even without appeal to religion, that cannot be one's fundamental stance, because it would be a failure to accept reality. It is not a healthy sign in our society that so many seek desperately to avoid the onset of age, and that death is a taboo subject. Death in fact and fiction is brought to our notice constantly on the television screen, but most Westerners do not integrate the thought of their own death into their outlook on life. Old age and death are part of the totality of a human life, which will only have its full richness if they are incorporated into it. It is a happy detail of English usage (one that is not paralleled in any other language that I know) that we speak of '*growing* old'. The whole of life is a becoming; and we do not cease to grow as persons even when our powers are declining. It is often only a person's death that enables us to appreciate fully all that their life has been. Somehow we become aware of the complete person in a way that was not possible at any given stage of their lives.

Although we may no longer have such an intense reaction to sensuous beauty as we had in youth, we can hope that we shall not become 'dried up' in old age. Immediately following that outburst in 'The Tower' against the absurdities of old age, Yeats wrote:

> Never had I more
> Excited, passionate, fantastical
> Imagination, nor an ear and eye
> That more expected the impossible.

The whole poem is concerned with the struggle between the passionate poetic gift and the ravages of age. The poet decides that the solution lies in the search for wisdom, which is also the theme of 'Sailing to Byzantium', in which he again stresses that this should not lead to dessication of soul:

> An aged man is but a paltry thing,
> A tattered coat upon a stick, unless

Soul clap its hands and sing, and louder sing
For every tatter in its mortal dress.

It is a lovely thing to see an old person whose soul claps its hands and sings. Even if we are not capable of lasting poetic song, we can share Yeats' hope when he wrote eight years later:

God guard me from those thoughts men think
In the mind alone;
He that sings a lasting song
Thinks in a marrow-bone.

(from 'A Prayer for Old Age')

A clear-sighted recognition of reality will make humans find some way of accepting the encroachment of age and the inevitability of death. For Eliot's 'apeneck' Sweeney, the whole of human existence could be summed up in three words: birth, copulation, death. That was all there was to it; and he didn't think much of it. But Sweeney's brutish attitude is not the only way of regarding the course of human life. One can find an almost aesthetic satisfaction in recognizing one's own journey from birth to death as part of the rhythm of all created being. This is particularly the case for anyone who lives in the country. The changing seasons give a pattern to daily life and activities. Vegetation and animals come into life, reach maturity, and in due course make way for the next generation. It can be strangely satisfying to feel oneself to be part of the rhythm of the vast respiration of nature.

So, on the non-religious level, we try to achieve equanimity and acceptance in the face of old age and death because they are part of the reality in which we find ourselves, even if there are still times when we resent the weakening of our powers. However, Etty Hillesum meant something more than I have said so far, when she wrote: 'By excluding death from our life we cannot live a full life, and by admitting death into our life we enlarge and enrich it'.

I return to the idea of *growth* into old age, but now in the light of Christian faith. Progress towards fulfilment in life is progress towards achieving true Selfhood; but this is very different from what many people have in mind in seeking 'personal fulfilment', which is largely concerned with the ego. The path of the human creature from birth to death can seem like the curve of a parabola. The child grows and develops its natural powers to become an adult person through experience and by relating to other persons. These powers reach their peak, and then comes what *seems* to be a slow descent down the other arm of the parabola into the diminishments of age and the ultimate emptiness of death. We have to develop the ego in order to become ourselves; but in the end we have, as it were, to 'give it away' in order to free the true Self. This is like the paradox that one can only develop fully as a person by giving to others, but there is nothing to give until one is a person. In fact, of course, the two developments proceed *pari passu*.

In the final analysis, there is a stark choice: the choice between God and the ego. God is our end, and we can only reach that end by going out from the ego-self to release the true Self for union with God. The gift of ourselves to others is a facet of our giving of ourselves to God. The desire of the ego is to possess and to control, which is limiting. We have been created to transcend such limitation, and this is achieved through self-giving. If this seems a negative way, it is very much for a positive end. Jesus put the choice plainly: 'Anyone loving his life will lose it, and anyone hating his life in this world will keep it for eternal life' (Matthew 16:24–5). We already have a beginning of that eternal life through the grace of partial union with Christ. It is what he came to give us: 'I have come that they may have life and have it in abundance' (John 10:10).

This whole journey is a movement towards fullness of life and of being. The human creature never really 'is' here on earth; he or she is always 'becoming'. When God says in the book of Genesis: 'Let us make man in our image', he is not speaking about an all-at-once creation. We have not *been* created; we *are being* created. When that creation is complete, we shall indeed be in the image of God. Our destiny is to be one with God. He has brought us from nothing that we may go to him, and we shall not be fully what we are intended to be until we have escaped from the limitations of the ego. Part of that process involves experiencing the diminishments of age. So Eliot, using 'are' in its fully existential sense, wrote in 'East Coker' III:

> To arrive where you are, to get from where you are not,
> You must go by a way wherein lies no ecstasy.

The rhythm of life consists of the positive and the negative, which leads to a further positive. There is the development of the person and his or her abilities, which are used to help to build up God's creation. Then comes the willing acceptance of the restrictions of age and the descent into the emptying of death, which is the gateway to the fullness of life. When he was already a mortally sick man, the composer Béla Bartók wrote: 'I came empty into the world, and I want to go empty out of it.' Bartók was an atheist, and he was referring to his hope of having time to say all that he had to say in music before he died; but it is a fine thought for any of us: to develop ourselves as fully as possible, to give all that we can to our fellow human beings, before being emptied to go to God. I suppose this rhythm of life is mirrored in the classical Hindu ideal of the four stages of life: the student developing mental and physical powers, the parent fully involved in family and social life, the hermit seeking and offering wisdom, and finally the homeless wanderer, detached from all earthly ties.

Just as we are most truly ourselves in this life when we give ourselves to God and to our fellow human beings, so we finally transcend ourselves by passing through the seeming diminishments of age to reach the climax of earthly life, which is death. (Paradoxically, that climax often appears to the watcher to be an insignificant moment: just a last exhalation of breath.) Death is the gateway to the eternal life for which we were created. It is a sort of birth, which is how the early Christians saw it when they called the day of a martyr's death the *dies natalis*. Unlike the martyrs, most of us will not have achieved the total gift of self to God by the time of our death; so that birth may be delayed, in some way that we do not understand, until the purification is complete.

The emptying of the ego is the one thing necessary to clear our way to God, and the glad acceptance of the weakening of our natural powers helps in this process. It is part of the positive growth towards God. 'Blessed are the poor in spirit, for theirs is the kingdom of heaven.' Human beings are essentially poor because they have nothing that they have not received. It is in the joyful recognition of our poverty that we meet God in this life; and it is in relinquishing what we think of as 'ours' that we approach the kingdom. The restrictions that come with age provide steps on that way. By transcending them we turn an apparent negative into something positive. Alas, it is easy to be impatient and ungracious, rather than welcoming; but it should be a cause for joy that into old age we can still be growing, growing towards our final destiny when we shall reach the fullness of our being in eternal union with God.

We cannot go to God unless we are holy, but holiness is not to have *achieved* anything. It is to be possessed by God. A human being is pure capacity for God. We are created from nothing, and in the parabola of earthly life we move towards maturity and then, seemingly, back to the nothingness of death. But in fact this is transformation into fullness of life. The transformation is painful at times because of sin; but one 'like us in all things but sin' has gone before us, suffering for our sins in the emptying, the kenosis, of the incarnation and the cross. As disciples of Jesus, we follow his way to life through death, from the cross to resurrection. The cross shows us that death accepted in love is the ultimate and deepest act of which human beings are capable. It is their final surrender to their God, when, like Jesus on the cross, they may echo Psalm 31 (30): 'Father, into your hands I commit my spirit'. The acceptance of the cross and of death as the gateway to resurrection into eternal happiness in union with divine love is the acceptance of the mystery of existence, as St Francis understood so clearly.

*

The Scriptures are God's revelation to humankind, transmitted in the words of human writers who lived in specific cultures and had their own mental outlook. In seeking to find 'God's meaning' behind those words we have to test them against our lived experience as well as in the light of the Church's tradition. Moreover, our faith that is rooted in Scripture becomes itself a factor in the interpretation of Scripture. We believe the wonderful revelation which the Gospels bring us through the words and life of Jesus, that God is love; and so we dare to interpret literally such Old Testament texts as the one in which God speaks with a love greater than that of a mother for her child. Human experience teaches us that love is vulnerable; and so, as I suggested in Chapter 9, it seems that God who *is* love must in some way be vulnerable, and that is the meaning of the cross. But if we rightly allow our human experience to be a factor in interpreting scriptural texts on divine love, we should not explain away other texts which speak of God's anger. I do not believe that it is correct to extrapolate from our experience of human nature to suggest, as Jung did, that there is a 'dark side' in God; but we cannot dismiss all the references in the Old Testament to God's anger as being merely anthropomorphic. Nor can we gloss over the uncompromising severity of Jesus' anger against those who refused to admit their sinfulness. So while we are comforted by the knowledge of God's love, we must never fail to recognize our total need of his mercy. There is no way that we of ourselves could dare to face God.

But that said, fortunately all that God in his mercy seems to require of us is that we acknowledge our sinfulness and our need of him. In the parable it was sufficient for the tax collector to say 'God, be merciful to me a sinner' to be able to go home at rights with God. As Julian of Norwich says, we are not capable of understanding the full evil of our sins, and yet God is ready to unite us to himself if we acknowledge our wretchedness. By his grace

> we may see our sin profitably without despair; for truly we need to see it; and by the sight we shall be made ashamed of ourselves and broken down as regards our pride and presumption; for it behoves us verily to see that of ourselves we are right nought but sin and wretchedness . . . He of his mercy limits the sight for us, for it is so vile and so horrible that we should not endure to see it as it is. And by this humble knowing, through contrition and grace, we shall be broken from everything that is not our Lord, and then shall our blessed Saviour perfectly heal us and unite us to himself. (*Revelations*, Chapter 78)

I know of no one who has ever expressed all this better than George Herbert:

> Love bade me welcome: yet my soul drew back,
> Guiltie of dust and sinne.
> But quick-ey'd Love, observing me grow slack
> From my first entrance in,

Drew nearer to me, sweetly questioning,
　　　　If I lack'd any thing.

A guest, I answer'd, worthy to be here:
　　　　Love said, You shall be he.
I the unkinde, ungratefull? Ah my deare,
　　　　I cannot look on thee.
Love took my hand, and smiling did reply,
　　　　Who made the eyes but I?

Truth Lord, but I have marr'd them: let my shame
　　　　Go where it doth deserve.
And know you not, sayes Love, who bore the blame?
　　　　My deare, then I will serve.
You must sit downe, sayes Love, and taste my meat:
　　　　So I did sit and eat.

God will accept us if we go to him empty-handed, relying entirely upon his love. Neither incompetence nor silliness nor admitted faults are obstacles, only the false self. We have to acknowledge the truth: that we are utterly dependent on him, that of ourselves we can do nothing. It is not any achievements that will count in the end (important though they may be in building up the individual and in what he or she is able to give to the world), but the handing over of ourselves to God so that our weakness and even our evil become steps towards him; and he will come to us in our emptiness:

Gott, dessen Wollust ist, bei dir, O Mensch, zu sein,
Kehrt, wenn du nicht daheim, am liebsten bei dir ein.

(Angelus Silesius)

*(God whose desire is to be with you, O human,/prefers to lodge in your house when you are not at home.)*

Some of the mentally handicapped seem to me to be close to God, and I think this is because they wear no masks, they have no pretences, they make no claims. They accept themselves and others just as they are. Unlike most of the rest of us, they do not need to get rid of any false self before they can go to God. I have the same conviction about many of those who have been defeated by life, the morally defeated who have lost all 'respectability' in society. They have true humility. They know that they must face their Creator empty-handed; and that is something which those who have achieved much in this life may have to learn in the stripping away of inessentials through death. The person who is truly aware of the evil that is in him knows experientially the depth of his need of a Saviour. There is a real sense in which God does not seem to mind about our sins, provided that we acknowledge them, that we recognize that we can do nothing without God, that we *are* nothing without him. Novelists such as Graham Greene and François Mauriac have written with insight about the deep Christian mystery that human beings are redeemed not only *from* their sin, but *in* their sin. The sinner knows that he cannot reach up to God, but God can reach down to him. The priest in *The Power and the Glory*, who through weakness cannot break a habit of sin, nevertheless loves God enough to give his life as a martyr, even though he has to get drunk to face his shabby and glorious death. Baudelaire, who made such a mess of his personal life, was perhaps 'not far from the kingdom', because he recognized that he could make no claim. During his life on earth, Jesus was accepted, not so often by the devout as by sinners who admitted their need. Looking at the cross, I know that I am accepted as I am. We can only go to Christ in our need, *because* of our need. In the parable of the great banquet (Luke 14:16ff.), it is the poor, the crippled, the blind and the lame who are eventually brought to the banquet, the symbol of the kingdom:

It's a long way off but inside it
There are quite different things going on:
Festivals at which the poor man
Is king and the consumptive is
Healed; mirrors in which the blind look
At themselves and love looks at them
Back; and industry is for mending
The bent bones and the minds fractured
By life. It's a long way off, but to get
There takes no time and admission
Is free, if you will purge yourself
Of desire, and present yourself with
Your need only and the simple offering
Of your faith, green as a leaf.

(R.S. Thomas: 'The Kingdom')

*

I am all at once what Christ is, ' since he was what I am, and
This Jack, joke, poor potsherd, ' patch, matchwood, immortal diamond,
Is immortal diamond.

These last lines of the Hopkins poem which I quoted at the end of the first chapter refer to the mystery of the transformation, through the power of the incarnation of God the Son, of a weak human being into one capable of union with God in eternal life.

From early Christian times a number of Greek Fathers used the term 'deification' to describe this transformation. This tradition goes back at least to St Clement of Alexandria in the second century, followed by St Irenaeus, Origen and others, notably St Athanasius in the fourth century. The idea was neatly expressed in the epigrammatic 'God became man that man might become God'. This doctrine has its basis in the New Testament, most explicitly in the late letter, known as the Second of St Peter, where the writer says that, through his gifts, God has made it possible for us to become sharers of the divine nature. St Paul expresses the same idea by saying that, as Christ is Son of God by nature, we too are sons of God by adoption, so that we can say 'Abba, Father', just as Jesus did, and we are destined to share his glory hereafter (Romans 8:15, Galatians 4:6). St John says: 'We are children of God now. What we shall be has not yet been revealed. We know that . . . we shall be like him because we shall see him as he is' (1 John 3:2). These New Testament writers are saying that already through grace we have begun to have, even in this life, a foreshadowing of that eternal life which implies being transformed into 'true images of his Son' (Romans 8:29). In our final union with God we shall have been made into that perfect image of himself that he had in mind in creating human beings. There is dramatic irony in Satan's words of temptation to Eve. In the first account of creation in Genesis, God communes with himself: 'Let us make man in our own image'. In the second account, after the description of the creation, Satan appears on the scene and promises Adam and Eve that 'you will be like gods'. He is echoing God's own words, for it is indeed God's intention that we should become like him; but that will not happen if we follow Satan's advice to try to set ourselves up as independent of God.

At the beginning of the *Paradiso* Dante coins a word to describe the transformation that is necessary in a human being in order to be made ready for union with God. He calls it *trasumanar*, a going beyond the human, something, he says, that cannot be described in words. In the course of the *Paradiso* Dante, as character, gradually transcends himself as he meets those who have already reached the eternal state of union with God. In trying to express the ineffable, he introduces a series of (not very elegant) neologisms (*inluiarsi, intuarsi, immiarsi, indiarsi*, to be inhimmed, inyoued, immeed, ingodded) to describe the completeness of the union. Dante achieves this union in the final lines of the poem, when his desire and will are totally united to Creative Love. This, of course, can only be a temporary union, since for the purposes of the poem, the pilgrim has to be able to return to earth to tell his story. His experience therefore corresponds to another meaning that was given to 'deification', namely the temporary mystical union that some, like St John of the Cross, attain for brief periods in this life. This meaning of deification became more frequent among the Greeks from the time of the fifth- or sixth-century writer known as Pseudo-Dionysius (because he published his work under the name of the Dionysius who became a disciple of St Paul in Acts 17:34), and was widespread in the medieval West through the influence of his mystical writings translated into Latin. In the twelfth century St Bernard used the term 'deification' in both senses. He considered it to refer essentially to the permanent state of beatitude in the next life, when the union of the human creature with its Creator will be like the state of a 'tiny drop of water mixed with a lot of wine which seems completely to dissipate when it takes on the taste and colour of the wine'. But he held that it was also possible for the mystic to experience fleetingly an analogous union in this life. It was surely because of his writings on contemplative union that the poet chose St Bernard to take Beatrice's place at the end of the *Paradiso*, to be the one who begs the Blessed Virgin for her prayers that Dante may be made fit for the total union of intellect and will (or, to use words of richer connotation, of mind and heart) with his Creator.

Dante emphasized that the experience of divine union was ineffable, not just because no words could be found to describe it, but more fundamentally because it was beyond terrestrial human conception. We simply cannot know what eternal life is like. It seems to me that in some way we shall enter into the eternal reality of our essential and total being in loving union with our Creator. That total being will include all that was positive but partial in the transient stages of our temporal life, not least all our love. Nothing will be lost. 'Deification' cannot mean the absorption of the human into the divine in any neoplatonic sense. In eternity the human being retains its existential integrity, but the human will is now in complete coincidence of love with the divine will, as Dante says in the last lines of the *Commedia*; and the human knower is now like God because he or she knows him as he is, as St John implies in the passage I quoted above. Having passed through the emptying of death and being stripped of the false self, the human creature is now, in love and in knowledge, a perfect finite image of its infinite Creator. All redeemed humanity will be united in God. We may wonder how many of the quirks of personality of those we love will be present eternally in their true Self. We cannot know; but since each one is a unique reflection of God, we can trust that there will remain all the individuality which we love.

*

One other consequence of our contingent existence in this world is that we need to learn to live provisionally because we have no certain security. We do not truly possess anything, neither external goods nor our abilities; and we shall not possess our true Selves until we have finally freed ourselves from the demands of the ego. Eliot in 'East Coker' III translates almost literally a maxim from St John of the Cross: 'Para venir a lo que no posees, has de ir por donde no posees' ('To come to what you do not possess, you must go by a way in which you do not possess', *Ascent of Mount Carmel* I 13).

To live in a provisional manner is to welcome each day as it comes; so a good motto is the Easter liturgy's exclamation taken from Psalm 118 (117): '*Haec est dies quam fecit Dominus . . .*', 'This is the day which the Lord has made; we rejoice and are glad'. We welcome what the day brings, its joys or its difficulties, because what each day brings is an opportunity for growth towards our final destiny of fullness of life. We do not know what may come in the future, and we may not always be able to avoid anxiety, but at a deeper level we can have confidence, because God will be there, not to protect us from possible sorrow or suffering, but to be with us in it and through it. 'I, Yahweh, your God, I am holding you by the right hand; I tell you, "Do not be afraid, I will help you" ' (Isaiah 41:13). The psalmist too quite frequently speaks of God leading him by the right hand; and a little further on in Deutero-Isaiah we have that lovely passage: 'Does a woman forget her baby at the breast, or fail to cherish the son of her womb? Yet even if these forget, I will never forget you. See, I have branded you on the palms of my hands' (Isaiah 49:15–16).

'This is the day' – even that is too long a span. The present *moment* is the only reality. It is in what has been called 'the sacrament of the present moment' that God is with us, whether we are standing enraptured by the beauty of nature or struggling with pain at the forefront of consciousness or in a neutral moment of no sharp awareness. We are in God's loving hands, and we can leave all to him. When we try to be conscious of God's eternal presence in our temporal present, we are again confronted by the mystery of the interweaving of absolute and contingent reality. This is the day, the moment the Lord has made. We rejoice in it because, whether it is a positive moment of achievement or a seemingly negative moment of diminishment, it is a step that brings us a little closer to our eternal reality. The great General of the Jesuits, Pedro Arrupe, was struck down by a massive stroke in 1980. Gravely incapacitated, he wrote:

> More than ever, I now find myself in the hands of God. This is what I have wanted all my life, from my youth. And this is still what I want. But now there is a difference: the initiative is entirely with God. It is indeed a profound spiritual experience to know and feel myself so totally in his hands, in the hands of this God who has taken hold of me.

*

In the first chapter I wrote about the paradoxical dual experience of our insignificance in this vast universe and of our immense personal worth, perceived in human relationships and – for Christians – as God's creatures redeemed by Christ. Our life on earth looks like a journey from nothing to nothing; yet God is at the centre of our being, and through the shedding of our illusory selves made possible by the life, death and resurrection of Christ we are destined, in the daring language of the Greek Church Fathers and of some mystical writers, to nothing less than deification. In that chapter I also recalled hearing Kathleen Ferrier singing Mahler's immeasurably sad farewell to the beauty of earth. That was at the Edinburgh Festival in the year before her death. A few years earlier in Oxford I had heard her singing another and very different farewell at the end of *The Dream of Gerontius*, the Angel's triumphant farewell to Gerontius, when he has passed through the bitterness of death and is about to begin the happy final purification which will bring him to union with his God. Only empty-handed shall we be able to approach the holiness of God. On the way we may find ourselves in darkness and rough waters, like the disciples on the Sea of Galilee, but we can hope that, like them, we shall finally hear the voice of Jesus: 'It is I; do not be afraid'.